Pelican Book A859

Archaeology LIAM DE PAOR

Liam de Paor is a lecturer in the history of civilization at University College, Dublin. He was born in Dublin in 1926 and educated there at Irish-speaking schools and at University College, from which he graduated in Archaeology and early Irish History. After a brief period as a cartoonist in a stained-glass studio, and two years' experience in architects' offices, he worked for over six years in the Office of Public Works in Dublin on the excavation and conservation of historic and archaeological monuments in the Republic of Ireland. He was also Executive Secretary of the Royal Irish Academy. Then for a year he acted as UNESCO adviser on archaeology and the protection of cultural properties to the government of King Mahendra of Nepal. For two years he did post-graduate research on Dark Age archaeology, mainly in Central Europe. In 1955 he married an archaeologist, and he is co-author with his wife Maire of *Early Christian Ireland* (1958).

Dr de Paor's interests tend to centre around his work, but this does not exclude his interest in the twentieth century and in current public affairs.

Liam de Paor

Archaeology

AN ILLUSTRATED INTRODUCTION

with drawings by Jane Mackay

 Penguin Books

Penguin Books Ltd, Harmondsworth, Middlesex, England
Penguin Books Inc., 3300 Clipper Mill Road,
Baltimore, Md 21211, U.S.A.
Penguin Books Australia Ltd, Ringwood, Victoria, Australia

First published 1967

Designed by Jane Mackay

Made and printed in Great Britain
by Hazell Watson & Viney Ltd
Aylesbury, Bucks
Set in Linofilm Times

Contents

List of illustrations

1

The beginnings of archaeology

An awakening of interest

We live in a world in which we are surrounded by the works of man. Countless generations of our ancestors, labouring to supply themselves with food and shelter and comfort, have transformed the face of the earth. We are made dramatically aware of man's conquest of nature if we consider the great machines which are now being sent out into space to photograph the moon and to enter into orbit around the sun, or the aircraft which travel daily from continent to continent, or even the great cities which have been built in all parts of the world; but if we remember that not only cities but the fields and woods of the countryside are the work of human hands, we may realize that indeed for several thousand years the greater part of the human race has lived in a man-made world. And we may begin to wonder how it all began and by what degrees the human race advanced to its present control of the forces of nature.

The later stages of the advance are clear enough. In the past two centuries men have accelerated the conquest of nature by means of science, in other words by the systematic observation and study of all natural phenomena. This study has been to a great extent the study of processes, the observation of what has happened in different sets of circumstances. Now man himself is a natural phenomenon, and as he has become more and more aware of the uses of scientific method he has felt it necessary to apply the same kind of scientific observation to himself, seeking to understand the processes of his own mind and his own society.

One of the oldest ways of doing this is through history, or through the traditional lore which is the primitive form of history. Every human society has preserved some traditions of its own past, and every society has to some extent explained itself in terms of its

The Acropolis, Athens

past, but it is interesting that Western civilization, which has been responsible for the development of natural science, has also, more than other civilizations, cultivated the study and philosophy of history. Two ancient cultures, both of which have greatly influenced our society, contributed to this. The first was that of ancient Greece. Of all ancient peoples, the Greeks were perhaps the most interested in man, and they made man the measure of all things. From one of their earliest writers, Herodotus, 'the father of history', our culture received the idea of history not as the self-glorification of a tribe or a nation but as an unbiased inquiring study of the affairs of men. The second was that of the Jews, the people of the Bible. The Jewish people contributed to us the idea of history as having direction, purpose, and meaning: in Butterfield's words: 'The God who brought his people out of the land of Egypt, out of the house of bondage, was to be celebrated in the Old Testament pre-eminently as the God of history.'

The records of the past, therefore, have always been one of the

The Great Pyramid

chief subjects of the inquiring western mind, but for many centuries, from Herodotus to Gibbon, the inquiry was limited to those periods and places for which written evidence is available. The Bible and the writings of the ancient Greeks and Romans for centuries provided what seemed to be the beginning of human history. No earlier writings were known, and therefore nothing, it seemed, could be known about the remote past beyond what had been preserved by the ancient writers.

But this limited knowledge seemed sufficient, throughout the Middle Ages and the early centuries of the Renaissance, to explain man's part on earth and his destiny. The inspired teachings and traditions of the Jews, as set forth in the Book of Genesis, told the story of the creation of the world and the fall of man and his loss of paradise. Pagan Greek and Roman traditions also told, in a less precise way, of a fall from a happier state – Hesiod speaks of successive Ages of Gold, Silver, and Bronze before the unhappy Age of Iron in which he himself lived – while the Christian teaching of the

Redemption gave a transcendental meaning to the whole story of the human race. After the Renaissance, learning became increasingly critical and increasingly concerned, in history as in other matters, to question established doctrines. The early results of this critical spirit were very various but on the whole did not depart seriously from the established view of human history. To take but two examples, Archbishop Ussher, on the one hand, by an analysis of the text of the Bible literally interpreted, calculated that the world was created in the year 4004 B.C. On the other hand, Gibbon, while in his great work he rejected the accepted view of Christianity's part in history, was still influenced by it, substituting, as it were, a secular *Decline and Fall of the Roman Empire* for the spiritual fall of man.

The Renaissance was a rediscovery not only of the writings but of the monuments of classical antiquity, and it brought about a general interest in the physical remains of the past. The artists and architects of the Renaissance took as their models the works of the Greeks and Romans, and they therefore studied these works more and more closely. Patrons of the arts, in Florence and then in Rome, began in the fifteenth century collecting antiquities to adorn their palaces and their cabinets. They were 'enjoyers' of art – dilettanti – and their tastes and collecting-habits gradually spread to other parts of Europe, while their desire of adding to collections of antiquities led in time to the purposeful exploration of famous sites of the Old World in the search for sculptures, coins, vessels of metal or pottery, and other *objets d'art*. Many of the great museums of Europe began as royal or princely collections in this manner. The custom reached its height in the eighteenth century and has continued to some extent down to our own day. It led to the systematic and comparative study of these classical antiquities. A German scholar, Winckelmann, in the middle of the eighteenth century, was the first to publish a comprehensive historical account of the art of the ancient world, based on the study of monuments and collections of antiquities in Rome and elsewhere. At about the same time, Englishmen, especially members of the Society of Dilettanti, were rediscovering the classical civilizations of the eastern Mediterranean and had begun to publish volumes on the antiquities of Athens and other sites in Greece, the Near East and Egypt. The antiquities collected in this period were not only small portable objects. Lord Elgin in the opening years of the nineteenth century bought (from the Turks) parts of the sculptured frieze of the Parthenon, the splendid temple of Pallas Athene, which he removed from Athens and transported to England, where he re-sold them to the

Winckelmann, 1717–68

A panel from the Parthenon frieze (Elgin Marbles)

British Museum. Similarly the French who invaded Egypt under Napoleon took an acquisitive interest in the antiquities of that country, although as a result of their defeat in the Egyptian campaign much of their loot also found its way ultimately to England. In the meantime, however, through the work of their Egyptian Institute in Cairo, they revealed to Europe something of the wonders of a civilization older than the Greek – that Egyptian civilization whose antiquity and mystery had already been a source of wonder to the ancient Greeks and Romans. The decipherment of the Egyptian hieroglyphic script, partly as a result of the fortunate French discovery of the Rosetta Stone (inscribed in three scripts) added a stimulus and provided a key for the study of ancient Egypt, and this study continued throughout the nineteenth century.

All this activity was of interest to an ever increasing number of people. In Europe the educated public was growing, and it was interested in all the discoveries that were being made and were leading to the formation of the modern world. Strange civilizations,

The Rosetta Stone

whether in remote parts of the world or remote in time, were of special interest to a society which had just begun to realize that it did not inhabit the centre of the universe. This background of interest gave its character to the Near Eastern exploration of the early nineteenth century. The discovery of ancient cities – especially those whose names were known from the Bible or other ancient writings – and the collection of museum-pieces were the aims of the explorers. Excavations were carried out in Egypt, in Asia Minor, in Mesopotamia, in Persia, and knowledge of past civilizations was greatly augmented. The excavations, however, were for the most part simply treasure-hunts: no effort was made to trace the growth and development of civilization from its beginnings, but simply to reveal works of art, architecture, and engineering which had been long forgotten. The main function these explorations served was to reveal that there were whole civilizations which had passed from memory or had survived in history only in a few mysterious names, and that the spade could uncover something of their vanished glories.

There was another aspect to all this activity besides the admiration for classical antiquity which had inspired the Renaissance. The curiosity of post-Renaissance Europe was boundless, and new discoveries were being made in every field: in astronomy, in geography, in natural history, in chemistry, in physics, in mathematics, and in art. Following the taste for the classical there developed the taste for the exotic. Chinese porcelain had already been imported into Elizabethan England, and a 'Chinese manner', especially in interior decoration, was much affected in eighteenth century Europe, while the art of the nearer Orient also had its influence on the arts and crafts – and indeed on the literature – of Europe. In this sense antiquity was simply one form of the exotic, and attracted the same kind of curiosity. Thus Nash, in designing the Brighton Pavilion, was inspired by the exotic, and created a pastiche of various oriental styles. Other early nineteenth century architects were inspired by antiquity and designed banks or public buildings which copied Greek or even Egyptian temples.

If a visitor to an art gallery looks at a fifteenth century Italian painting of, say, the Crucifixion, he will observe that the scene is rendered with Italian fifteenth century costumes, furnishings, and landscape: if he then turns to a nineteenth century painting of the same subject he will see that the painter has tried to reconstruct accurately a Palestinian scene of the first century. It was antiquarian discoveries which supplied the necessary information for this, and

18

Martin, Belshazzar's Feast

the word 'archaeology' is used in just this sense by Oscar Wilde in an essay on theatrical costumes and props. There was a mid Victorian fashion for paintings which attempted this sort of reconstruction for its own sake – the mid nineteenth century painter Martin may be cited as one of many examples. Through such paintings, and through historical novels, the discoveries of archaeology and of history were given shape and interest for the public at large. There was therefore a quite considerable demand for new discoveries and publications on ancient civilizations; a general public support intensified the efforts of nineteenth century explorers of the ancient world.

The development which has just been sketched was the work of men who were interested not so much in their ancestors by blood as in their spiritual or intellectual ancestors, men who thought of themselves as the heirs to the civilization of Greece and Rome. Their point of view is well expressed by an historian, Lord Acton: 'A speech of Antigone, a single sentence of Socrates, a few lines that were inscribed on an Indian rock before the Second Punic War, the footsteps of a silent but prophetic people who dwelt by the Dead Sea and perished in the fall of Jerusalem, come nearer to our lives than the ancestral wisdom of barbarians who fed their swine on the Hercynian acorns.'

19

But there was another point of view, held by people who were interested in the pre-Roman ancient monuments of their own lands, or in their ancestors or predecessors in those lands – the 'barbarians': Ancient Britons, Gauls, Iberians, Celts, or the Germanic tribes who dwelt beyond the Rhine in the Hercynian Forest. This romantic interest in the past also dated back nearly to the Renaissance; for the rise of scientific archaeology it was perhaps even more important than the interest in classical antiquity. It was in fact not wholly distinct from the study of classical antiquity; in part it was the poor man's substitute for classical antiquarian researches – which required expensive journeys to the Mediterranean lands for their pursuance – and at first it was just as dependent on the writings of classical authors. All the obviously pre-Roman monuments which were still to be seen in the landscapes of western and northern Europe were attributed without discrimination to the barbarian peoples whose names were known from these writings. The growth of nationalism contributed considerably to studies of this nature, and sixteenth century England was one of the first places where it flourished. The office of King's Antiquary existed at this period, and a short-lived Society of Antiquaries was founded in the reign of Elizabeth I. Camden's *Britannia,* a topographical and antiquarian work, which was published as early as 1586, was the first classic of this school of antiquaries. Antiquarian studies and writings of the same sort increased and flourished in the seventeenth and eighteenth centuries, societies wholly or partly interested in the study of antiquities were founded, and although the antiquarian movement remained dazzled by the light of classical literature and was unable to penetrate the gloom of prehistory, it did much valuable work in the recording of antiquities – especially field antiquities – as they were in the days before the whole landscape of Europe was altered by the effects of the Industrial Revolution.

The names of Edward Lhwyd, John Aubrey, and William Stukeley are especially notable in this period in Britain. Stukeley in particular, in his careful and methodical recording of field antiquities, anticipated the scientific approach which modern field archaeology demands. He prepared accurate drawings and descriptions of many monuments in Britain including the great prehistoric temple of Stonehenge: today these serve as valuable records of the state of the monuments more than two centuries ago. In his views Stukeley exemplified the fascination which the Druids – the Celtic learned and priestly caste who are described by Caesar, Tacitus, Diodorus Siculus, and others –

20

Drawing of a Druid by Rowlands
Stukeley's Plan of Avebury, 1724 (over page)

A British Druid

Chindonax Britam
24 Feb. 172?

Stukeley delineavit

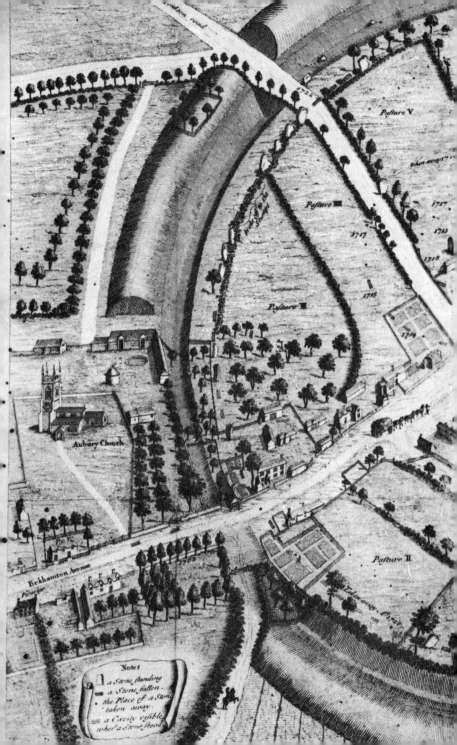

Pasture V

Pasture III

Pasture II

Pasture II

1717
1717
1718
1718
1718

1713
1718

1724

Aubury Church

Bckhamton Avenue

1762

Notes
a Stone standing
a Stone fallen
the Place of a Stone
taken away
a Cavity visible
where a Stone stood

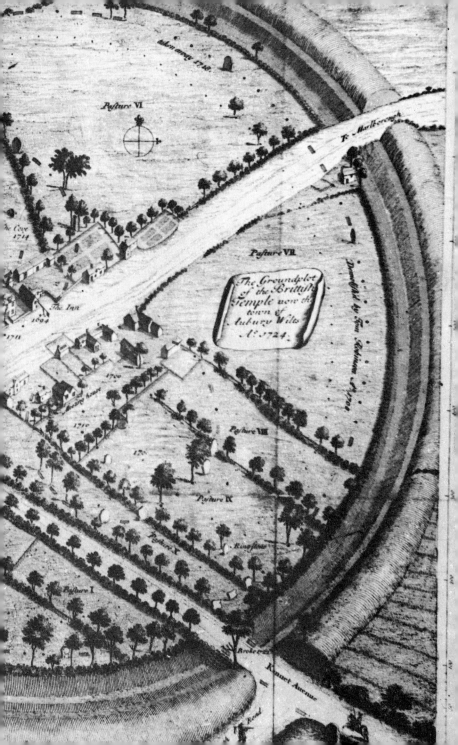

exercised on the imagination of the Romantic period, and which caused an astonishing variety of monuments to be attributed to them.

On the Continent antiquarianism took a similar course. There too collections were made of 'barbarian' as distinct from classical antiquities, and prehistoric field antiquities were recorded. While the aristocrat added to his collections by bringing back trophies from the Mediterranean, the physician or the schoolmaster interested himself in the prehistoric burial mounds or 'rude stone monuments' of his own parish, and published accounts of them. These early antiquarian records often acquired a fortuitous value through the subsequent destruction or loss of the antiquities themselves. The history of the tomb of Childeric I, a king of the Franks who died in A.D. 481, provides an interesting example of this. The tomb was discovered and opened in 1653 in Tournai, and its extremely rich contents – jewelled weapons, personal jewellery, and other grave-goods – were incorporated in the collection of the Royal Cabinet of Louis XIV. They were stolen from the Cabinet des Médailles in 1831, and although some of the objects were subsequently recovered by the police from the Seine, most of them were lost. The contents of the grave had however been fully published, with careful scale draw-ings, in 1655 by Jean-Jacques Chifflet, a physician, and, since the rich grave-goods are of considerable importance in the study of early Germanic art in Europe, the 1655 publication is still much used today.

Engraving (1655) showing objects from the tomb of Childeric

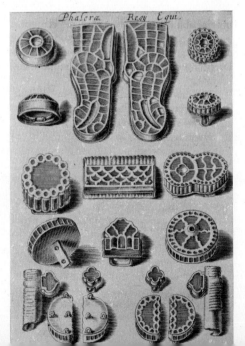

The development of chronology

One chief difficulty beset the researches of the early antiquaries: they had devised no means of distinguishing earlier from later prehistoric antiquities and were obliged uneasily to discuss the most heterogeneous objects and monuments as if they were contemporary. The first steps towards solving this problem were taken in Denmark in the early nineteenth century. At the beginning of the century the antiquarian collections of the Danish National Museum were already sizeable, and in 1816 Christian Thomsen was appointed first curator of the Museum to look after them. Following ideas which had already been expounded in Scandinavia, he divided the collection into three parts, containing respectively implements of stone, bronze, and iron. This, he claimed, was not merely a convenient and rational arrangement of a mass of varied material but was a representation of the successive stages of improvement in material culture through which man had passed. It had the advantage of being an arrangement which justified itself: in itself it argued for the truth of Thomsen's view. After a long tenure of office, Thomsen was succeeded by his pupil and assistant Worsaae, who continued to expound and develop his ideas. The truth of the idea that man had progressed from the use of stone for his implements to the knowledge and use of bronze and then of iron was capable of demonstration in the field, and was so demonstrated by excavation. The views of Thomsen and Worsaae were soon known outside Denmark and, after some controversy, they prevailed generally, so that the 'three-age system', first adopted in Copenhagen, became the basis of prehistoric chronology, as it still is to this day.

This idea of the three ages was in the spirit of the views on evolution and progress which were coming into being from the late eighteenth century on. Thomsen had devised his scheme specifically to deal with the problems of Danish prehistory and had not claimed that his suggested Scandinavian chronology was of universal application; nor was there any suggestion of a very high order of antiquity for the museum objects in question. But the method he adopted was to bring archaeology into close relationship with a science whose discoveries at about the same time provided the occasion for a great nineteenth century controversy. This science was geology.

The study of the rocks and soils which make up the crust and surface of the earth had shown that a great many of these consisted of sedimentary deposits, that is of material which had settled down from solution or suspension in water. The formation of vast thicknesses of consolidated rock by any normal process of sedimentation was one which could not be envisaged occurring in the space of a few thousand years, but any interpretation which involved attributing great antiquity to the earth was repugnant to the pseudo-chronology derived from the Bible. Many geologists escaped the dilemma by suggesting that the deposits were the result of a series of catastrophes, of which the latest was the Biblical flood. In the eighteenth century this 'catastrophic' or 'diluvial' theory was already being challenged. Its opponents argued that the processes which had formed the rocks were still going on and could be observed and that the uniformity in character and in speed of these natural processes, in the past as in the present, should be admitted. They argued furthermore that the record of the rocks could be read by observing the stratification of the sediments, the earliest deposits being overlain by, and therefore lower than, the later. But the nineteenth century was well advanced before these new views began to prevail.

In the meantime human bones or stone objects obviously of human manufacture were being found in increasing numbers associated with bones of extinct animals or sealed between layers of stalagmite in caves. Such finds inspired people here and there in various parts of Europe to carry out systematic researches in cave deposits, and from the beginning of the nineteenth century onward claims were made from time to time to demonstrate that man had lived at a very remote period, as a contemporary of the rhinoceros, the hyena, and the mammoth in Europe. For long all such claims were disbelieved or ignored. Two very assiduous workers whose researches were thus unrecognized were Dr P. C. Schmerling, who spent many years in the early nineteenth century exploring, in conditions of great difficulty and discomfort, caves near Liège in Belgium, and Father MacEnery, who at the same time was excavating in Kent's Cavern near Torquay.

The vindication of these and other workers had to wait until after the mid century. A customs official of Abbeville, Jacques Boucher de Perthes, had spent about twenty years collecting, exhibiting, and claiming as 'antediluvian' chipped flint implements from the gravels of the Somme, before his claims were investigated and finally admitted by French and English scientists in the years 1854–9. His triumph then, however, was complete: the Institut in Paris and the Royal Society in London, among other learned bodies, accepted his proofs of the antiquity of man. In the same few years two other important events occurred: Darwin published in 1859 his *Origin of Species by Means of Natural Selection,* and in 1857 the bones of a man whose skull differed considerably in form from a modern human skull were found, together with flint implements, in a cave at Neanderthal in Germany. New ideas and new discoveries in the 1850s, therefore, brought about a revolutionary change in archaeological research. The vast scale of geological time was becoming clearer, the period in which man had been living on earth and manufacturing implements was now admitted to be very great, and the idea that man might have evolved from lower forms of life by means of natural selection was at least being investigated.

The Neanderthal skull

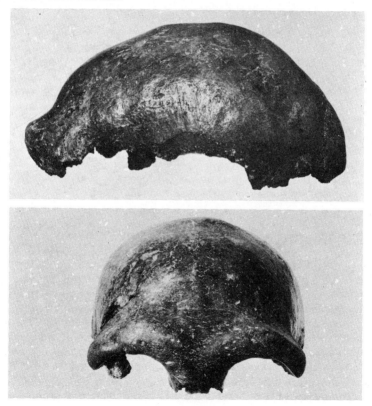

This revolution in thought, combined with the Danish three-age system, was so effective in providing both stimulus and scope for antiquarian research that it may be considered the beginning of pre-historic archaeology as a learned discipline. The framework of a prehistoric chronology was supplied by the three-age system, the scale of the chronology was at least indicated by the geological back-ground of the finds of fossil human bones, and the method necessary for archaeological study was already available in part in the geological principles of stratification and association. It now became clear that the Ancient Britons, Gauls, and others to whom all prehistoric antiquities had previously been attributed were simply the peoples who had occupied the stage at the very end of prehistory, and that they were preceded by many peoples who must remain nameless or be given arbitrary names purely for the archaeologist's convenience in discussing them. It also gradually became clear that the three-age system was not in itself sufficient to express the stages through which man had passed in his long prehistory. Further subdivision became necessary, especially in the immensely long Stone Age. At first two main phases were distinguished in this, but it is as well to anticipate here and give the main subdivisions as finally concluded: Lower, Middle, and Upper Palaeolithic (Old Stone Age, down to the end of the geological Ice Age), Mesolithic (Middle Stone Age, in the early post-glacial Period), and Neolithic (New Stone Age, characterized by the beginning of agriculture). These are not strictly speaking periods of time, but successive phases of culture, whose absolute date in years will vary from one part of the world to another, while whole phases will be absent in some parts of the world.

Archaeology today

It was a long time before this distinction became clear, and European prehistory suffered, and still suffers to some extent, from an over-concern with subdivision into 'epochs'. The three ages, of Stone, Bronze, and Iron, for example, having proved so useful in providing an opportunity to establish a prehistoric chronology, were then taken as having an absolute and universal value in themselves, as significant and meaningful in their way as the mythical Gold, Silver, Bronze, and Iron Ages of Greek tradition. These divisions still tend to be over-emphasized today, although it is clear that in Europe, for example, the distinction between the Neolithic and the Mesolithic is far more significant, culturally, than the distinction between the Stone Age and the Bronze Age, while the distinction between the Middle Bronze Age and the Late Bronze Age is similarly more significant than that between the Bronze Age and the Iron Age.

But prehistoric archaeology is still a new science, and one with diverse origins. Most of the methods and concepts to be described in the next chapter are the result of the work of the century since 1859, and development has been very uneven in different parts of the world. Classical and Near Eastern archaeology has revealed, through large-scale excavation, the character of ancient civilizations in considerable detail. On the other hand, on rich urban sites, the stimulus was lacking to bring about the perfection of precision techniques in archaeological investigation. These techniques were forced on European prehistorians by the very difficulty of the sites and material with which they had to work. In general, problems of chronology have so overshadowed European prehistory for the past century that the broad study and understanding of human culture and civilization have suffered, until recent years. In a way, the most interesting developments have been in America. There the historical approach has been much less in evidence than in Europe, and archaeology, on the whole, has been an extension into the past of social anthropology – partly because many of the prehistoric cultures of America are still available for study today in the Indian communities which are descended from them and preserve their customs. As a result, American archaeologists have developed techniques and concepts for the study of prehistoric cultures which are worthy of more attention in Europe.

The most striking, although not perhaps the most important, development in archaeology in recent years has been that more and more scientific techniques, especially for dating, have become available to the archaeologist. Less striking, but probably more significant, has been the gradual replacement, more or less within living memory, of the amateur by the professional archaeologist. Most of the principal universities of Europe now give degrees or diplomas in archaeology, and although the antiquarian societies and the amateur investigators still exist, and indeed do valuable service both in the work they do and in helping to keep archaeology on the side of the humanities, the archaeologist is now as intensively trained and as professional as the chemist or the engineer.

Stonehenge (top) *and the Amphitheatre, Troy*

2

The methods of archaeology

Discovering the site

The archaeologist's object is no less than the study of mankind, but he may be forgiven if occasionally he loses sight of this. For he must spend a great deal of his time like a rag-and-bone merchant picking over the oddments in rubbish pits. As diligently as Sherlock Holmes devoted himself to the minute study of cigar ash, he examines potsherds, broken implements, decayed stumps of timbers, crumbling foundations, or the contents of graves. For in dealing with prehistory he has available to him only the evidence of such unpromising remains as these in his effort to form a picture of vanished societies. And like the detective he must reconstruct past events with clues – with the traces left by human activity on the material world – and he must prepare time-tables and compare theories to see which best fits the facts. But the past events he reconstructs are the life of a whole society; the time-tables he prepares are on a scale not of hours but of centuries. For in archaeological research – and in this prehistory differs most strikingly from history – the individual can rarely be isolated from his society. Man in prehistory is anonymous: archaeology tells nothing of the deeds, still less the thoughts or words of great men. Social groups, not the individuals who composed them, are the subject matter of archaeology.

'First catch your hare' begins the recipe for hare soup, and clearly the first task of the archaeologist wishing to study the remains of early man is to find them. Broadly speaking, antiquities are found in three ways: some because they are obvious; some because someone who knows how to set about it looks for them; many simply by accident. The obvious field antiquities are buildings or artificial mounds or other earthworks whose origin and purpose are clearly not of our day. Long before the beginning of scientific archaeology it

31

was recognized that many types of field monuments were ancient, but they were often attributed to the people of dim and distant historical periods. Inigo Jones, for example, reported that Stonehenge was a Roman construction, and many earthworks in the British Isles were thought, for no good reason, to be the work of the Danes.

When an active interest in material antiquities developed, the early antiquaries began to theorize about the more puzzling ancient monuments, and soon, in an effort to understand them, they went on to dig in them. Even in its crudest form excavation was, in effect, an application of the scientific principle of putting hypothesis to the test of experiment. Were the 'rude stone monuments' druids' altars? Repeated experiments in the form of excavation showed that many of them were in fact tombs. As a result of many such experiments, the archaeologist today can classify most of his field monuments, and knows, more or less, what most of them are. He also knows approximately when many of them were erected, but this knowledge is the result of more elaborate research than the simple test of excavation. For many important archaeological discoveries were made unmethodically, and sometimes, like Columbus's discovery of America, by men who did not know what it was that they found. 'I have looked upon the face of Agamemnon,' reported Schliemann, to choose an example which is by no means an extreme case, when he uncovered a golden death-mask in one of the Mycenaean shaft-graves, and had in fact revealed a rich civilization centuries earlier than that of the Homeric heroes. It was only when the earlier excavations had yielded their full supply of museum objects that classification of the material could begin and its full significance begin to be revealed.

There are many antiquities in the field which are not immediately obvious but which can be identified by the skilled searcher. This is especially true of monuments which have been all but destroyed. A few stones built into a modern wall may reveal the previous existence of an ancient structure, an unusual configuration of field fences that of an ancient earthwork. A stretch of a modern highway whose line is carried on straight across country by narrow lanes or field boundaries may indicate the site of a Roman road. The study of large-scale maps can be of great help to the worker who seeks to discover such almost vanished sites, but photographs taken in suitable lighting conditions from the air can reveal an astonishing number of traces which are simply not visible at all from the ground – faint mounds or hollows which show up in a slanting light, or slight changes of colour in crops which may indicate ancient disturbance of the ground. Sometimes

*Heinrich
Schliemann,
1822–90*

Mycenaean gold death-mask

tradition or historical evidence may provide at least a hint at the
position of an ancient site. The Mycenaean was not the only civilization which that remarkable nineteenth century German, Schliemann,
discovered. Taking Homer as his guide, believing that the Iliad was
at least in part historical, he set out to find the forgotten site of Troy.
He decided that a mound at Hissarlik in Asia Minor was the place,
dug there, and uncovered not only Homer's Troy but a whole series
of cities which had been built and rebuilt on the spot.

Finally, a great many ancient sites and objects whose presence is
revealed by no surface indication are found accidentally. When road
or railway cuttings are being made, when gravel is being quarried,
when trenches are being dug for drains or foundations – even when a
farmer is ploughing a field – antiquities may come to light which have
long lain hidden and unmarked in the earth. It is probably true to say
that most of the objects now housed in the museums of western
Europe are the result of such chance finds.

33

The sorts of evidence

Field monuments, and the implements and weapons which are found from time to time, provide direct evidence of man's activity: they are artefacts: they were made by man. Less direct evidence is also available. A skeleton in a Bronze Age grave is not an artefact, but the fact that it was buried in crouched position supplies some information on human activity. To take a more subtle example, a grain of carbonized wheat found on a habitation site of the Stone Age in England is also not an artefact; but it may provide information not only on the food of the inhabitants of the site but also, indirectly, on movements of population and culture, since wheat is a cultivated plant which is not native to England. Archaeology therefore has two main classes of evidence to deal with: things made by man, and circumstantial evidence of human activity or custom.

In this evidence, on which the study of the prehistory of the human race must be based, there are serious gaps. While a bronze axe or a flint arrowhead, for example, will survive for thousands of years in most soils, the wooden shaft of the arrow, except in unusual conditions, will perish, and an iron axe may rust away into dust. Or social customs may vary greatly in the evidence they leave for archaeology. If a society buries its dead in stone-lined graves, then it will leave a clear record in the earth for the archaeologist to find and study; if it has the custom of exposing the dead to vultures and hyenas, then the bones will be carried away and scattered, and the material evidence will be considerably less clear. Furthermore, it is only some kinds of human activity which leave traces that the archaeologist may find at all. Thus, we may expect to find evidence for prehistoric painting and sculpture, but we cannot hope ever to have much information on prehistoric song.

To some extent archaeology has made virtues of its necessities. If it must work mainly with the débris and trivia of human culture – with the pots and pans, the lost buttons and broken pins – then it will endeavour to extract as much human information from them as Sherlock Holmes from cigar ash or Dr Thorndyke from dust. If it is deprived of the opportunity to study men as individuals, then it will study them statistically, and work with abstractions to achieve results which need only a little imagination to breathe the human spirit back into them.

The abstraction thus imposed means that although the ultimate

Food vessel from Four Knocks, Co. Meath, Ireland,
showing detail of seed impression

object of study is man as a social being, the methods used are akin to those of the material sciences, and a great deal of archaeological work is taken up with the measurement and analysis of purely physical data. As in the natural sciences, classification of data is of primary importance. It should already be clear that all the miscellaneous evidence available from the past must be arranged in some sort of order before interpretation can begin.

Excavation alone, even if unmethodical, can serve to show which types of field monuments mark the site of a grave, which the site of a dwelling, and so on; in other words it can provide a rough classification of monuments in the field. However, it is the study of the objects found, together with scientific methods in excavation, which makes it possible to tell the date of a monument, its significance, and the culture to which it belongs. The basis of archaeological research therefore is the slow patient work of classification of objects in museums.

Classifying the finds — typology

Artefacts — man-made objects — are classified in three principal ways: according to function, according to date, and according to culture or context. Functional classification is usually a necessary preliminary to chronological study. Thus all the axes, all the pots, all the swords, and so on, in the collection or from the region being studied are gathered, each forming a single group. Chronological classification within each group can then follow.

When Thomsen divided the antiquities in the National Museum of Denmark into three main groups of stone, bronze, and iron implements, he took the first important step in the chronological analysis of museum material. His divisions were based on certain characteristics of the objects (in this instance the material of which they were made) which seemed to him to be of cultural or chronological significance. The chronology thus established was relative not absolute: Thomsen's analysis showed that the Stone Age was earlier than the Bronze Age, and the Bronze Age earlier than the Iron Age; but it did not in itself reveal at what date in years any of the three ages began.

From such a simple threefold chronological division of a large number of miscellaneous objects it is possible to proceed to further subdivision, and a great deal of archaeological research involves the refined classification of groups of objects according to the principles and methods of typology. Typology is the arrangement of objects and their study in significant groups (or types) which show development or degeneration in form or function. The whole method depends on what might be called the principle of the observed rarity of innovation, or in other words, on the conservatism of human nature. For although men have freedom of choice in their actions, it is a freedom severely limited by environment, by social prohibition, by custom, and by the sheer inertia which simplifies all activity. Men tend to make things, if not rigidly to a pattern, at least in a style to which they are accustomed, and by and large drastic changes in the shape of things made come about gradually. The mason carves his stone in the way he learned as an apprentice, and thus the student of medieval architecture can tell by the appearance of the ornamental mouldings on a church doorway whether the church was built in the thirteenth or in

the fifteenth century. This 'inertia', this conformity to the spirit of his own age and time, applies even to the most self-consciously original artist – so that the expert eye can judge the date of a building or a painting of this or of an earlier century. Things of everyday use are easier, and their date can often be judged even by the inexpert eye. It does not require any special training or skill to tell a pre-war motor car from a recent model, or to recognize in, say, a group photograph the fashions of the 1920s or the 1930s.

The motor car, indeed, provides quite a good example of a typological development. The earliest 'horseless carriages' faithfully followed the form of the horse-drawn carriage of the late nineteenth century and were only slightly modified to accommodate the new means of propulsion. As time went by, motor cars gradually lost the lines of the horse-drawn carriage, became more streamlined, to operate efficiently at the higher speeds of which they were capable, and were built longer and lower in proportion. This is a development governed in the main by improvement in function, and is an illustration of the principal sort of typological series with which the archaeologist has to deal. A series of types may, however, simply

37

result from gradual changes of fashion or taste. This is largely true of changes in types of clothing, of types of personal ornament, and often of types of pottery, although function plays its part in these changes also.

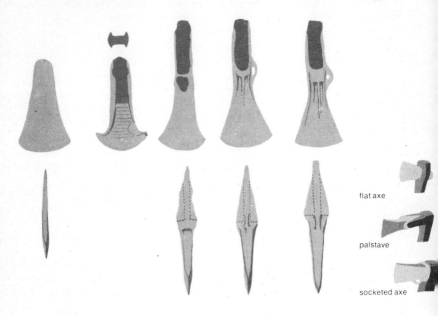

Typology of the copper and bronze axe

A classic example of a typological series in the prehistory of the British Isles is provided by the development of the copper and bronze axes. The earliest axes were of stone, and the polished stone Neolithic axe (at the top of page 101), mounted in a pierced haft, suggested the form of the earliest metal axes. These were of copper, and were rather massive, with narrow blades like their stone proto-types. But flat axes were soon cast. These were more economical of metal, and were just as efficient since the new material was stronger and heavier than stone. In use, however, the thin butt of the axe would tend to be driven back into the piercing of the haft and to split the wood. This difficulty was met by casting a 'stop-ridge' at the narrowing of the blade, to prevent the butt from wedging back into the haft. Finally, this stop-ridge was gradually enlarged, and the edges of the axe were first hammered and then cast into projecting flanges, until a pocket was formed on each face of the blade. With the developed form a new and more efficient hafting system was used in which a forked piece of wood was employed, the shorter arm of the fork being split to take the axe-butt and the split ends firmly lodged in the two pockets. This developed axe, which is known as a palstave, was often equipped with a cast loop, so that it might be further secured by binding back to the haft. Finally, in the Late Bronze Age, socketed axes came into general use, although these were not developed from earlier types in the British Isles but were introduced from outside. The typological development of axes has a chronological significance, flat axes of copper or bronze appearing in the Early Bronze Age, palstaves in the Middle Bronze Age, and socketed axes in the Late Bronze Age. But axe types provide only a very coarse chronological framework. To be closely datable, objects must belong to what are known as 'sensitive types'; that is types which quickly reflected changes of fashion and preferably are neither durable nor long-lived in themselves.

For this reason pottery is a very useful index to the archaeologist. It is easily broken, so that no one pot is likely to have been in use for a very long time, yet, although the pots are short-lived, the material of which they are made is among the most durable and will survive

La Tène brooches

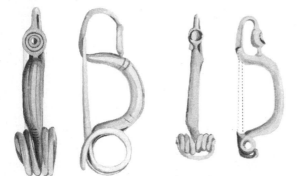

well in most soil conditions. Pottery is also a medium in which changes of fashion are easily and quickly reflected, and at least in early prehistoric times its fragility precluded its being exported or transported over long distances, so that it can usually be taken as a local product of the area where it is found. Sir Flinders Petrie, by studying the changes of style in pre-Dynastic Egyptian pottery, was able to arrange the contents of prehistoric Egyptian graves in a chronological sequence, thus establishing a relative chronology for the pre-dynastic periods. He called this method, which was based on the typology of pottery, 'sequence-dating'.

Refinements of typological analysis depend largely on the study of objects found in association. In effect this means the study of groups of objects found together in circumstances which suggest that they were all in use at one and the same time. Very often the contents of a grave will fulfil this condition, where a man or a woman has been buried with some of his of her personal possessions – weapons, personal ornaments, or objects of everyday use. A 'hoard' may also serve – that is, a group of objects deposited together (usually by

Pottery types: Neolithic (top) *and Bronze Age*

someone who had the intention of recovering the objects later). But the mere fact that a group of objects was deposited by one man at one time is not a certain indication that the objects were all in contemporary use. Many hoards, for example, are of the type known as 'founders' hoards'. These consist of broken metal objects, gathered by a purchaser or collector of scrap for the purpose of melting them down and re-using the metal. Such a collection may contain some objects centuries older than others. Again, the mere fact that things were found together in a deposit does not necessarily mean that they were all deposited at one time. At some periods, for example, especially in the Early Iron Age in northern and western Europe, it was customary to make religious offerings (usually termed 'votive offerings' although they were not necessarily all of this character) at certain sacred places, by throwing valuables into a pool or marsh at a particular spot. Such a custom could extend over a great number of years, and offerings of various dates will then be found in a single large group in the mud or peat of the marsh bottom.

Late Bronze Age hoard from Calbe, Kr. Schonebeck, Saxony

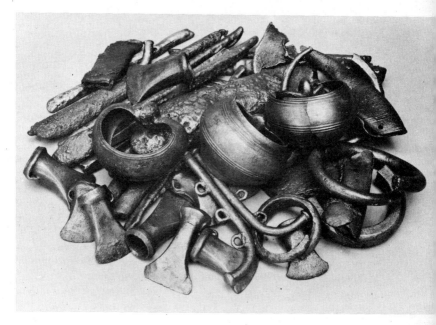

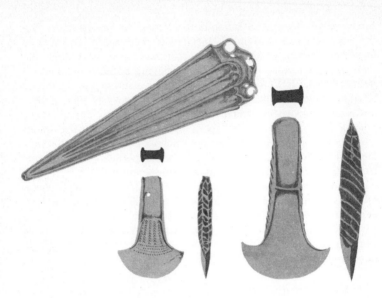

Early Bronze Age hoard containing flanged axes, Great Britain

When due precautions have been taken in identifying the character of associations, and when a large number of associated groups is available, then typological study can proceed to establish a relative chronology. When the Bronze Age hoards and grave groups of the British Isles are studied, it is seen that flat axes sometimes occur in association with palstaves, and palstaves are sometimes found associated with socketed axes, but flat axes are not found together with socketed axes. This provides the simplest form of typological series, with three types, of which Type A continued in use after the first appearance of Type B, and Type B continued in use after the first appearance of Type C, but Type A was already obsolete before Type C made its appearance. It will readily be seen that three is the minimum number of types or phases for a typological series. It should also be immediately apparent that in the example given, Type B is represented by the palstave; but a moment's reflection will show that, solely on the association evidence given, it would remain uncertain whether Type A was represented by the flat axe or by the socketed axe. In other words, pure typological study will show the arrangements of types in a series, but it will not necessarily reveal the

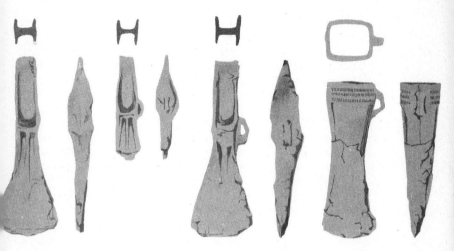

Late Bronze Age hoard with palstaves and socketed axe, Great Britain

direction of the development. So far as metal axes are concerned, there is a logical functional development which indicates that the axe was evolving in the direction of greater efficiency. But devolutionary series do occur, and some external check or control is necessary to show the direction of typological development. Axes, for example, occur in hoards with many other types of object – daggers, halberds, knives, swords, and so on – which in themselves provide some sort of control, while the flat axes at one end of the series are clearly related to polished stone Neolithic axes and the socketed axes at the other end of the series are occasionally found copied in wrought iron, so that there can be no doubt which is the earlier and which the later.

By typological analysis of large numbers of associated objects (mainly in grave groups) chronological frameworks were built up at the turn of the century for the European Bronze Age – by Montelius for the west Baltic area and by Reinecke for Bavaria and Central Europe. Similar chronologies have been worked out by the same methods for other periods and places. But for archaeological study in general, especially in the Near East, the most important method for establishing relative chronologies has been excavation in the field.

Planning and recording an excavation

Chronology is by no means the only object of scientific excavation. Archaeologists dig to find their material in its context. They seek in the ground, not gold, valuables, or inscriptions, although they may sometimes find these, but information about past cultures. To extract this information from the soil demands knowledge and skill, and the mere plundering of the ground to recover objects of beauty or curiosity is not archaeological excavation. The excavator's task is to uncover the traces of the human past methodically, and methodically to record and interpret what he finds, both on the site in his notebooks and drawings and then in print, so that the evidence may not be lost. The responsibility of making full records, and publishing them, arises because excavation destroys the evidence.

The approach to excavation varies according to the site, but the methods and principles employed, whether on a great tell compounded of the accumulated débris of a whole sequence of oriental cities, or on a muddy lakeshore where mesolithic savages built their camp fire, are basically the same. What traces remain of the structure or layout of the site must be carefully disentangled from the soil which has engulfed them, the remains of different periods must be distinguished, and all the finds must be recorded three-dimensionally.

'How do you know where to dig?' is a question which the archaeologist is often asked. There is no single answer to it. It will already be clear to the reader that many forms of archaeological site reveal their presence at a glance to the experienced or even to the inexperienced eye – in the form of earthworks or stone structures. Others are less immediately obvious but may still be located by means of surface indications. Ancient field systems, roads, or tracks may be discovered by careful observation; other sites may reveal themselves by faint markings which are visible only in special conditions of light or from the air. But the presence of many sites is discovered by accident, often through the finding of antiquities by the ploughman or the road-builder.

More rarely the archaeologist may rely simply on oral tradition or written documents in 'knowing where to dig' when there are no surface indications or when it is a question of choosing one site from among many of the same kind. There have been some successful instances of exploratory excavation, and Schliemann's justification of his belief that Homer's Troy was a real place and that he knew

44   *Woodhenge from the air*

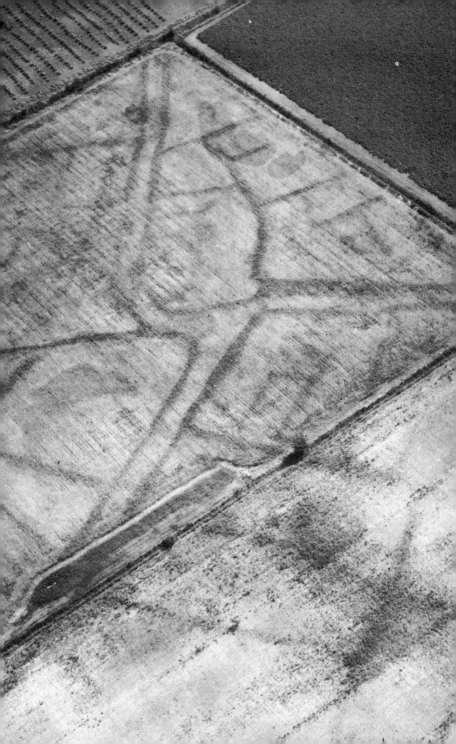

where it was added a chapter not only to the history of archaeology but to the history of mankind.

Having chosen his site, the archaeologist begins – and this in itself is an indication of the primary object of scientific excavation – by making the first part of his record. He notes the position of the site in relation to natural features and to other ancient sites. Then he records the condition of the site itself before excavation, by descriptive notes, photography, and three-dimensional survey. Only when the preliminary records have been made does he proceed to the laying out of the main lines of the excavation itself. This is a planned operation. An archaeologist who knows his business will no more proceed to dig haphazardly than a skilful butcher will hack at random at a carcass of beef.

The plan of the excavation will depend upon the nature of the site. The ruins of a city, a burial mound, a system of Bronze Age fields, each presents its own special problems. Broadly speaking, so far as layout is concerned, the main special cases which require special treatment are structures, burials, and caves. Most other types of site require 'area excavation' – the digging of a finite and usually arbitrary area which will include a sufficiently large and representative part of the site.

In laying out the site the excavator's object is to render the digging itself, the removal of excavated material, and the full recording and interpretation of evidence as easy and as economic as possible. Thus he must ensure that the dumps of excavated material from his first cuttings do not prevent or obstruct later cuttings if it should become necessary to extend the area of excavation. To facilitate recording he must plan his cuttings so that they will be roomy enough for ease of working and ample access of light, avoiding deep cramped ill-lit trenches. Since his records must be made in three dimensions he will leave himself as much opportunity as is expedient to preserve sections as well as plans of the remains. In an area excavation this is most commonly achieved by setting out a grid pattern of squares of equal size, each with an unexcavated margin. The size of the squares will be determined by the depth to which it is expected digging will be necessary. In prehistoric habitation sites in the British Isles, for example, it would be unusual to encounter archaeological deposits extending more than six or seven feet below the present ground surface, and with depths of this order squares of ten feet in Britain or three metres in Ireland (where archaeologists employ the metric system) would normally be the unit of the grid. The sides of the

Crop marks showing ancient field systems near Spalding, Lincolnshire

Surveying team at work

squares actually excavated would be eighteen inches or thirty centimetres less than this, so that as excavation proceeds the site assumes the appearance of a great chessboard, with square holes separated by narrow balks.

Such a layout has great advantages. In the first place, in itself it imposes some order and method on the excavation. It makes surveying and recording on plan easier, because the squares supply a framework of reference within which the parts of the site can be readily identified and correctly plotted in their relations one to another. It simplifies supervision, since one worker can be made responsible for each square. It facilitates the removal of excavated material and access to all parts of the site, since the balks form a network of paths

The Van Giffen 'quadrant' section. (The excavated areas are in grey)

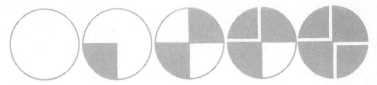

An earthen barrow

for barrows and supervisors. Finally it makes available a large number of vertical sections: each of the four sides of each square, which are cut as cleanly vertical as the soil conditions will allow, provides a section through the stratified deposits.

Not all excavations, nor even all area excavations, follow this pattern. It is unsuitable for many types of monument and site. A refinement of it, the 'quadrant method', devised by the Dutch excavator Van Giffen, is much used in the excavation of circular barrows and other small mounds. The diagram shows the stages by which, when this method is employed, the mound is totally removed. It will be observed that one of the objects of the method is to preserve to the last moment two full cross-sections.

The history of the site – stratigraphy

The emphasis which excavation methods place upon the preservation as long as possible of vertical sections arises from the archaeologist's duty to discover not only the nature but the history or chronology of the site. If he is excavating a house-site, for example, he will wish to know whether the house had been occupied for a long time or a short time, whether it had been reconstructed, and if so how often, whether there had been any significant cultural changes during the period of occupation of the site and in what order they occurred, and so on. To answer these and similar questions he depends to a considerable degree on the principle of stratigraphy. This was the method employed by the geologists to read the record of the rocks at the time when scientific archaeology was coming into being. It is based on the fact that in an orderly sequence of deposits the later will overlie the earlier. This obviously applies to deposits of human as of natural origin, and the operation of the principle can be observed in any city street where a deep cutting has been made for laying cables or drains. Glance into the cutting while it is open and you will see at the top the paving of the street, below that probably a number of layers of earlier paving, below that again perhaps rubble filling, and at the bottom, if the cutting be deep enough, the natural soil which underlies the town. When a vertical section is cut through a prehistoric site a similar sequence of layers is often revealed. Especially in any town, inhabited continuously over long periods, the ground level tends to rise over the centuries, because of the steady accumulation of débris of all sorts and the repeated re-paving of streets and rebuilding of houses on the one site. The section shows the accumulation stratified, layer upon layer, the objects and materials found in the several layers reflecting the changes of fashion and of culture which have taken place in the history of the site.

The interpretation of stratigraphy, however, is by no means always, or even commonly, a simple and straightforward business. Extreme complications enter into even the natural strata studied by geologists, because of movements of the earth's crust which distort or displace the layers in the rocks, or because of volcanic action below the surface which may insert sills of igneous rock between older sedimentary strata or may cut clean across the stratification with intruded dykes of lava, or because of erosion of the surface by water and weather, which may remove or modify exposed layers.

Barrow excavation at Earls Farm Down, near Amesbury,
showing layout to give four cross sections

Section profile showing stratification (the dark layers indicate habitation levels)

Archaeological strata, exposed not only to the natural forces of erosion but to the unpredictable activity of man, are even more liable to complication. The men and women who inhabited an ancient site may have dug pits, they may have dismantled old buildings to obtain materials for constructing new ones, they may have levelled a site for a house by clearing away the remains of a previous occupation, they may even, in filling up a hollow place to make it level, produce a reversed stratification by using old occupation débris as their filling material, drawing first on the upper layers as being the nearest to hand, which will become the lowest layer in the hollow, while the lowest layers of the old material, being the last to be reached, will be the topmost part of the fill. But apart from such complications as these the identification and interpretation of archaeological layers – the 'reading' of a section – on most sites is a difficult matter, and one which requires experience and training.

The vertical sections are the index to the history of a site. Guided by them, the excavator must try to recover that history by removing the significant layers one by one from the surface of the site, peeling off in reverse chronological order the layers which represent successive phases of culture or occupation, and recording fully all the evidence in the form of finds or traces of structure or activity which pertains to each phase. That this is a process which demands skill and knowledge will be appreciated when it is remembered that the excavator is destroying his evidence as he goes. If he fails to observe and record as he proceeds he will have no opportunity afterwards to make good his omission. He may recover objects of interest in themselves – and generally will be pleased if he does so – but if he wants to study interesting objects he can do so with much less trouble and expense by visiting a well-stocked museum. The objects found in a

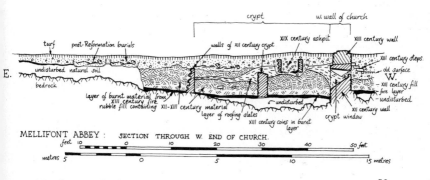

Simple stratification: a section drawing showing phases of destruction and re-building in a medieval abbey church

53

properly recorded excavation, however, are of far more scientific value, whatever their intrinsic merit, than those of unknown provenance and context which form the bulk of so many museum collections. The importance of association for typological study will already be clear, and good evidence of association is available only where the circumstances of finding have been accurately recorded.

Re-creating vanished structures

Information, not plunder, is the object of excavation, but the finds are not to be despised: they form an important part of the information. And if the excavation is skilfully conducted, finds may be made which would pass quite unobserved by the untutored digger for treasure. No one, however unobservant, could fail to remark the presence of a stone building in the earth if any substantial parts of the walls or foundations remain, but the plan of a prehistoric timber house, the wood of which has long decayed away, will not be revealed by the careless spade. Yet it has become a commonplace for archaeologists to recover detailed information on wooden buildings the structural material of which has wholly perished. This is done by carefully peeling and scraping away the accumulated strata on the site, by constant sweeping and cleaning of the excavation, and by observing all changes in the colour, texture, and firmness of the soil. The simplest and commonest illustration is provided by post-holes which have revealed the plans of so many vanished buildings – ranging from Upper Palaeolithic shelters and Neolithic farmhouses to Roman barracks and Saxon halls. When a building is constructed of a framework of timber posts, these will usually be sunk in the ground for stability. After the destruction or decay of the structure the parts of the posts which are above ground will collapse and rot away on the surface, or be carried away leaving no trace. The short lengths of post embedded in the ground, however, will decay in the ground. To the excavator their presence is revealed by patches differing in colour and texture from the surrounding soil. By emptying such post-holes – carefully spooning out the darker or softer material until only the surrounding soil is left – or by cutting sections through them he can ascertain whether the posts had been standing erect or set at a slope, and this information will help to decide the form of the structure of which they were a part.

A Neolithic hut site showing post-holes and pits (top)
(Slieve Breagh excavation, 1961)
Remains of wooden houses at Fedderson Wierde

Traces of the Sutton Hoo ship

Some of the most delicate tasks in excavation, comparable to the developing of a photographic negative, involve the discovery of the form of structures or objects which have decayed away. The former existence of hurdle work in a Neolithic burial mound in England was detected by careful excavation which revealed the impression of the long-vanished hurdles on a vertical face of the substance of the mound; skilful shaving of the sandy soil under Bronze Age barrows in the Netherlands has exposed, as a mere faint stain, the shadowy forms of the skeletons whose bones had been eaten away by the acid sand; guided at the outset simply by faint discolorations in the sand, the excavator of the rich Sutton Hoo ship burial went on, in an operation of extreme delicacy, to shave away the sand which had filled the buried ship until he came to the corroded nails which had clenched the ship's planks, then to feel for the slight change in the consistency of the sand which revealed where the decayed timbers had been, and so to remove all the filling until 'the face of the excavation everywhere was the sand which had pressed against the timbers of the boat from the outside, and which sometimes still bore in recognizable form the imprint of the grain of wood', and to recover full and accurate information on the dimensions and construction of a vessel whose substance had disappeared. Small objects of perishable materials can present similar problems.

Silhouette of a body in Tumulus II, Elp, Netherlands

Sir Leonard Woolley's acute observation enabled him to provide solutions to such problems in excavating graves at Ur. One grave revealed its presence simply by two holes in the ground, which Sir Leonard recognized as the cavities left by the decay of an organic substance. Liquid plaster of paris was poured into the cavities, where it set and assumed the form of the vanished uprights of a harp. With further delicate treatment of the other parts the whole form of the harp was revealed, together with its ornamental mountings. And at the same site the form of the elaborately ornamented and inlaid sledge-chariot of Queen Shubad, the whole wooden structure of which had long collapsed into dust, was recovered by even more painstaking and delicate treatment of the mosaics, inlays, and mountings which lay loose in the soil.

Queen Shubad's sledge-chariot

Plaster cast of a wooden harp, Ur

Problems for other specialists

Timber and other organic materials do not always decay away. In very dry conditions or in airtight waterlogged conditions they can survive for many thousands of years, but they still present a problem to the excavator. A wooden object, for example, removed from peat or mud which has preserved it, will rapidly lose its shape on exposure to the air, unless it is specially treated. Excluding the air and keeping it wet will serve as a temporary emergency measure, but the care and treatment of perishable, fragile, or corroded objects are matters in which the competence of the archaeologist as such is severely limited. In many technical aspects of his work the archaeological excavator

Excavating a cinerary urn

is in the position of the person who has an elementary knowledge of first aid: he is not a surgeon or a physician, and must be ready to consult with or hand over to an expert in another field if the occasion arises. In digging into the soil at all he has entered the province of the geologist and the soil-scientist; in so far as he must deal with bones he must acknowledge the superior status of the anatomist, the zoologist, the physical anthropologist; when he finds evidence of the plants which sustained or hindered early man he must become a client of the botanist; when he encounters problems relating to buildings and structures he must defer to the architect and the engineer. On

Prehistoric corpse from a bog

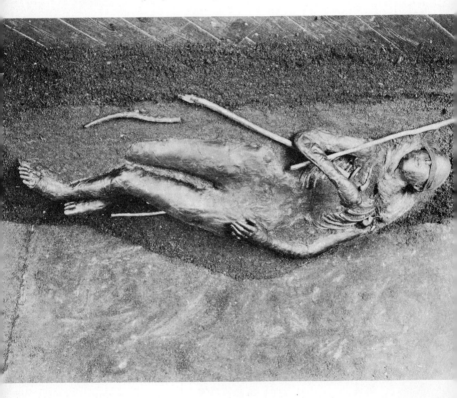

excavation sites (especially in the Middle East) where inscriptions may be expected, and indeed may be of vital importance in the interpretation of the evidence, the archaeologist must consult the epigraphist, who may well indeed be an important member of his staff. Archaeology deals with so wide a range of human activity – especially, because of its peculiar limitations, with the more practical forms of human activity – and with so much of the natural world which affected and was affected by that activity, that at every turn the archaeologist will find a specialist better qualified than himself to pronounce upon some aspect of his work.

Inscribed clay tablet from Knossos

Four scientific dating processes

The contribution of the natural sciences has been especially important to archaeology in establishing the chronology of the prehistoric past. It was the science of geology which first opened up the vistas of prehistoric time by establishing that the deposits in which remains of Palaeolithic man had been found were of an age far greater than the Biblical. Since then, more precise and refined dating methods have been devised for natural events and processes of the past twenty thousand years or so, to which the remains and traces of human activity can be related by archaeological methods.

(1) As long ago as the late nineteenth century Baron de Geer of Stockholm observed that the geological history of Scandinavia after the end of the last Ice Age could be read in lake muds and clays in Sweden. When the great ice sheets which had covered much of northern Europe began their slow retreat northwards, as the result of the gradual melting of the southern fringes of the ice, they did not withdraw in a smooth uninterrupted movement. Melting took place in summer; in winter the retreat paused. The melting produced lakes and pools which contained fine clayey material which had been gathered up and embodied in the ice. This material settled to the bottom of the lakes as silt, the coarser grains being deposited first (during and immediately after the summer melting), the finer settling down through the cold still water in winter. A thin layer, or 'varve', was thus deposited each year, each varve being graded from coarse at the bottom to fine at the top. In large lakes a number of these varves were superimposed; they also overlapped, each one stopping at the winter limit of the ice in the year it was laid down. Variations in the thickness and texture of the varves reflected minor climatic fluctuations from year to year. No single lake is wide enough or deep enough to display a sequence of varves covering the full retreat of the ice, which continued for thousands of years, but since any given sequence of years can be identified in a varve section by its particular pattern of climatic fluctuation it was necessary only to locate a sufficiently large number of overlapping sections to establish a full chronology. The diagram illustrates the principles of the method. This Baron de Geer succeeded in doing in the early years of the present century, when – to quote the title of his paper – he provided 'A Geochronology of the Last 12,000 years', by which it became possible to date the various stages of the ice retreat in Scandinavia and the various

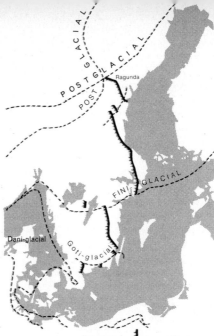

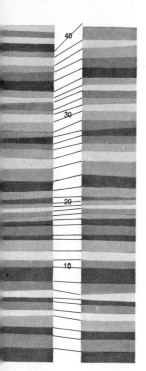

------- Ice margins ▮ varve sections

Two sample columns of varve deposits (left) *and varve section showing deposition of varves in four successive years*

The map (above) *shows ice recession and varve countings in Sweden according to de Geer. The varve sections are shown to cover almost the entire distance from the Dani-Gotiglacial moraine to Lake Ragunda*

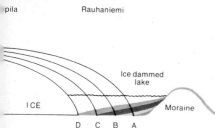

changes in the relative areas occupied by land and water in the Baltic region consequent on the release of vast quantities of water from the melting ice and the simultaneous removal of the tremendous pressure of great thicknesses of ice from the earth's crust. Wherever archaeological remains could be related to any phase of the ice-withdrawal or of the changing coastline, they too could be dated by the varve-counting method.

(2) Another counting method, similar in principle, is based on the fact that trees grow by adding a ring – clearly discernible in cross-section – to the trunk every year, and that the growth rings of trees, like the clay varves, reflect minor climatic fluctuations. It is obviously possible to determine the age of a felled tree by counting the growth-rings, and within any single climatic area the sequence of thick and thin growth-rings in a number of trees will give a pattern which reflects fluctuations of climate (especially of wet and dry years) over a given period. Where a sufficient number of overlapping sequences is available it is possible to work back from modern timber to the beams incorporated in old structures and so to work out the pattern of minor climatic fluctuation over long periods. Ancient beams and timbers can then be dated, by seeing into which phase of the full

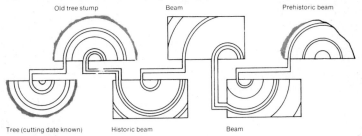

Schematic drawing of a series of wood sections illustrating cross dating and showing how a chronological sequence is built up to connect prehistoric timber with modern trees

sequence the pattern revealed by their growth-rings will fit. This method, known as dendrochronology, is of more recent development than geochronology or varve analysis, and so far it has been applied most successfully in America, especially to the dating of Indian villages. In Europe its results are promising, although in its application it is limited to structures or sites containing reasonably large beams. To obtain an absolute date in years, it is of course necessary to have a full sequence pattern of overlapping examples from the object to be dated right down to the present day, but a long series which is not tied to an absolute date can provide an accurate relative dating for timbers from different sites which fall within the period covered by the series. It will illustrate the possibilities of the method in Europe to say that only one gap remains to be filled before it will be possible

The Oseberg ship

to give an absolute date to the famous Viking ship-burials which have been found around Oslo Fjord, and that only two comparatively short gaps remain to be filled to provide dendrochronological dating in England back to the first century B.C.

(3) Atomic physics has made available a chronological method of wider application in archaeology. As a secondary effect of the bombardment of the upper atmosphere by cosmic rays from outer space, some atoms of the nitrogen isotope N14 are converted into atoms of the carbon isotope C14, which is radioactive. This radio-active carbon mixes with the ordinary carbon (C12, with a small proportion of C13) contained in the carbon dioxide of the atmos-phere. Carbon dioxide is absorbed by plants, which sustain animals and men, so that carbon is incorporated in all living organic matter.

The proportion of radioactive carbon (C14) to ordinary carbon (C 12) in the world carbon reservoir is considered to be constant, and the proportion absorbed by living organisms is the same as that in the atmosphere. Once an organism dies, whether it be plant or animal or man, it ceases to take in carbon. The C14 contained in it, however, is *radioactive*, that is it decays (reverting to nitrogen) at a steady rate. The rate is expressed in the half-life of the radioactive element; that is the time it takes for half of the original quantity to decay. The half-life of C14 is about 5,600 years. Dead organic material, therefore, incorporates an atomic clock, ticking away the centuries as its radioactive content decays at a constant rate. The date at which an organism died, therefore – the date for example at which the tree was cut down from which a piece of wood derives – can be measured by comparing the proportion of C14 to C12, in the sample being dated, with the proportion of C14 to C12 in a modern control sample, and by using the known half-life of C14 to calculate the age of the ancient sample.

There are difficulties in radio-carbon dating. The proportion of C14 in atmospheric carbon is extremely small, and the instruments necessary to make the measurements are elaborate and costly. Fission and nuclear bomb explosions in recent years have introduced a new, artificial, source of C14 in the atmosphere, which must be reckoned with. Since the Industrial Revolution, modern industry has had an opposite effect by adding to the atmosphere a great deal of dead carbon (which has lost its radioactive content) through the use of fossil fuels such as coal and oil. Because of this, the usual practice now is to use a modern control sample which is more than a century old. There are other sources of error, arising principally from the effects of processes in the living organism and of bacterial action on the dead organism. Finally, the assessment of the age of an ancient sample is complicated by the fact that although the rate of decay of radioactive carbon is statistically constant over a very long period, there are wide short-term fluctuations, so that the result arrived at must be expressed as a statistical probability. An age determined by the radio-carbon method is expressed in the following way (the figures given here are quite arbitrary, for purpose of illustration): 5,000 ± 300 years. The figure 300 here is not a margin of error but a standard deviation, and the meaning of the expression is that the true age of the sample probably (66 per cent probability) lies within the range specified, and very probably (93 per cent probability) lies within twice the range.

Radio-carbon dating, in spite of the difficulties and the irreducible errors in the method, has already provided a useful chronological framework for the past 10,000 years. For dates earlier than this, the reliability and value of the method fall off considerably. It is a framework of absolute dates in years, the approximate accuracy of which has been tested by independent methods. Even if there is still an error in the absolute dates provided, the radio-carbon method provides a reliable relative chronology, independent of place or of cultural connexions, which can be of very great value to the archaeologist.

(4) Yet another science which has been called on for dating the past is botany. In certain conditions, especially in bogs and marshes, the grains of pollen shed by trees and other plants will survive, preserving their form, for thousands of years. Pollen is wind-borne and so is spread widely over the countryside, and it is produced in abundance by trees. Quite a small sample of pollen grains taken from the surface of a bog, when it is examined and the various species identified and counted under a microscope, will give a rough indication of the proportions in which various species of trees occur in the woodlands for a wide distance around. If a growing peat bog be dug into, and a sample taken up from three feet down, the analysis of the pollen found will give the proportions of different species in the tree growth when the bog surface was three feet lower than its present level. If it be remembered that there was a time, long after man had appeared on earth, when a great part of northern Europe was covered by ice, beyond which there extended for hundreds of miles a waste of treeless tundra, it will be realized that on a good site the pollen stratified in a deep bog will give a rough outline of the history of the vegetation of the area, showing which species of trees first appeared after the withdrawal of the ice, and how the forest and plant growth changed in composition from period to period. Now, the main factor influencing the floral and arboreal composition of a region is climate, so that vegetation history is indirect evidence for climatic history.

Since climate is the main influence governing the composition of the vegetation, the pollen from different sites in a single geographical region will tell a similar story, although there may be minor divergent features due to local conditions. The palaeobotanist who is studying vegetation history, as revealed by pollen, chooses his site, and with a drill takes samples of the soil or peat, of standard size and at fixed intervals of depth. The samples are washed in the laboratory to free the pollen grains from the substance in which they are embedded, the grains of each species represented in each sample are counted, and each species is then plotted, for every separate sample or level, as a percentage of the total tree pollen from the same level. A graph is then drawn, which reveals at a glance the changing character of the forest. When enough sites in the region have been examined in this way, the pollen diagrams from the different sites may be compared, and it will be seen that they all tell more or less the same story; and if some of them tell only a small part of the story it can readily be seen where they fit into the general sequence. An archaeological object found in a bog or in pollen-bearing mud can be assigned its place in the sequence. Where the climatic and vegetational phases revealed by the pollen diagrams can be dated, as they can in Scandinavia by their association with varve deposits, an approximate date is supplied for the object.

Palaeobotanical research has been carried out in most parts of northern Europe, notably in Scandinavia and Ireland, where it has been intensive. The climatic sequence revealed is broadly similar all over north-west Europe, and in each large region the pollen diagrams are divided up into zones corresponding to the major climatic phases since the Ice Age. In Ireland, for example, the chief periods generally recognized are a Late Glacial period, immediately

Pollen grains (left)

A pollen diagram (right)
of Clonsast, Co. Offaly,
Ireland, showing how a
track in a bog is dated to
the medieval period by
means of pollen analysis
NOTE: *Corylus and*
Quercus in the diagram
read from right to left

following the withdrawal of the ice sheet which had covered most of the country, a period which was extremely cold and characterized by open landscapes with sparse growth of willow and birch; the 'Pre-boreal Period', dry and cold but showing a slow improvement of climate and the beginnings of forest growth; a long 'Boreal Period', dry and cool, in which the land became thickly forested and bogs began to develop, pine woods spreading rapidly; a wet, windy, and cool 'Atlantic Period', in which hazel spread rapidly and mixed forests of oak and elm flourished; a dry and warm 'Sub-boreal Period'; a wet and warm 'sub-Atlantic Period', and finally a period covering modern historic times, in which the widespread clearance of the forest by man and his deliberate introduction of exotic species are reflected in the diagrams.

In a very broad and general way the results of pollen analysis can supply a dating, especially for objects of types which are not suscept-ible to close archaeological dating, such as dug-out canoes found in bogs, but vegetation phases which in a general way reflect climatic phases cannot in themselves supply a precise or refined chronology. In many areas the dating of pollen zones is rather decided by the archaeological objects which are found in them. Furthermore some

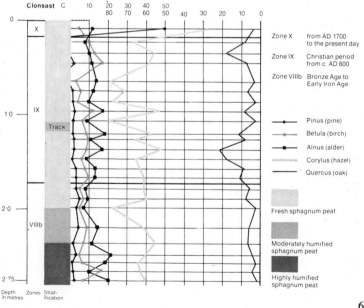

69

zone boundaries are better defined than others, and the transition (for example) from the Atlantic to the Sub-boreal Period, at which the Neolithic of the British Isles makes its first appearance, is particularly ill defined and cannot be used for close dating. The provision of absolute dating is not, however, the only, or even the chief, use of pollen analysis in archaeology. It is by supplying a picture of the pre-historic landscape that this botanical method makes its principal contribution to the study of the human past. The pollen from an archaeological layer can tell a great deal about both the natural vegetation and the plants introduced by man in the vicinity of the site, at the period which the layer represents, and this botanical information, combined with the information supplied by the study of animal bones on the site and of plough marks, ancient fences, or other direct evidences of human activity, may help to reconstruct a very detailed picture indeed of the economy of a past human society. How detailed the picture may be is illustrated vividly by the work of Professor Clark and his colleagues on a camp of Mesolithic hunters at Star Carr in the north of England, and by the work of a group of Scandinavian scholars on the site of an Iron Age village at Vallhagar on the island of Gotland in the Baltic.

Maps in archaeology

Every one of the methods so far described has involved in some degree the setting of the archaeological material in its context of time or place. The study of the geographical context employs several other methods. All archaeologists use maps, almost as much as geographers do and for very similar reasons. Before he can really study a prehistoric people, the archaeologist must first be able to identify them. This he does by recognizing the significant groups of objects which distinguish this group of people in particular from other peoples. Now, if he plots on a map all the places in which such significant objects have been found, he should at once have a fairly good idea of the area which was occupied by the people he is studying. But archaeological distribution maps, like other methods, have their own pitfalls which must be guarded against.

In the first place the archaeologist, in plotting a group of objects or monuments on a map, must be sure whether they are all of the same kind; or if they are not, he must be clear as to what they have in

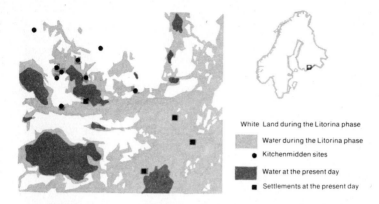

Dwelling places of the Ertebølle or Kitchen midden culture on the ancient shores of the Litorina sea in South Finland

common. Are they, for example, all of approximately the same date? If they are not, the map may give a misleading picture of the situation at any given moment of time. Are they objects which were made and used in the home or are they the products of a trading or exporting industry? Does the known distribution really reflect the situation in ancient times or is it affected by the activities of collectors in certain areas or by other modern activities? These and other questions must be asked before the evidence of maps can be handled with confidence.

A few examples will serve to illustrate the function of different types of distribution maps in archaeology. The distribution of a 'culture', that is of a group of people behaving, so far as the archaeological evidence goes, in significantly the same way, is usually revealed by plotting on a map the find-places of the various objects or monuments which are taken to be distinctive of the culture. An interesting illustration is provided by the map of coastal sites of the south Scandinavian culture known as the Ertebølle or 'Kitchenmidden' Culture. These sites are defined as dwelling places of the Ertebølle people by a whole range of finds of typical objects, including pottery and flints, and by the character of the sites themselves. They follow not the modern coastline of the Baltic but the old coastline of what is known as the 'Litorina Sea', at its maximum about 5000 B.C. Provided there is available a sufficient range of distinctive types, and provided enough investigation has been done in the field, it is – in theory at any rate – comparatively easy to define the distribution of a culture.

When it comes to distributions of single types, difficulties and complications enter the picture. The map here reproduced shows the distribution of a particular (and very distinctive) type of pot – the Beaker, of Neolithic and Early Bronze Age times in Europe. In human terms what does this map represent? Not the area of a single culture, for Beaker pottery appears in different cultural contexts, being associated in some parts of Europe, for example, with pre-metal economies and in other parts with metal-using economies. Nor would the old idea that the spread of this pottery type marked the spread of a race of people – the 'Beaker Folk' – now be generally accepted. The map may, however, be a guide to the movements of early traders or prospectors, and may mark the spread of a new type of economy in Europe – trading combined with pastoralism. Long-distance trade, once it makes its appearance in the economy, pro-duces of course another type of distribution, that of objects traded.

Distribution of Beakers in Europe

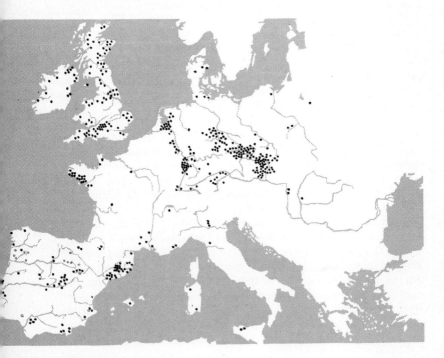

Gold lunula from Cornwall

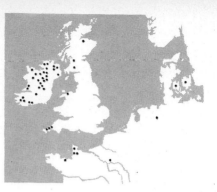

Distribution of lunulae in Europe

Distribution of axes of Graig Lwyd stone in Britain

Graig Lwyd

Two examples will serve to illustrate this. The first shows the distribution in Europe of crescentic sheet-gold ornaments known as *lunulae*, which are dated (chiefly because of the character of the incised ornament they bear) to the Early Bronze Age. It will be seen that the greatest concentration is in Ireland, with a scatter across Britain and north-west Europe, the type being represented in England only in Cornwall, which is as it were a 'stepping-stone' between south-east Ireland and the Continent. It would be rash, however, to assume that the main concentration on a map always represents the area of manufacture. Even in prehistoric times manufacturing for an export market rather than for home consumption was not unknown. The second map shows the distribution of identified specimens (identified by petrographic analysis) of axes of Graig Lwyd stone in the British Isles. Here the centre of origin, a quarry site in North Wales, is known, but the map gives an idea of the extent of long-distance trade in at least one useful commodity in Neolithic times.

73

When certain other features besides the location of archaeological monuments or find-places are marked, the map may supply information on the habits or economy of early man. A suitable geological map, used as the basis of a distribution map, may for example show which types of soil were sought or avoided for prehistoric settlement. When the early Neolithic settlement sites of Continental Europe are plotted on a soil map they are seen to concentrate on areas of the fine, light, wind-deposited soil which is known as löss. In Britain, what has been defined as the primary Neolithic culture is concentrated on the areas of chalk, but here one may suspect a pitfall, for most of the types represented on the chalk are paralleled (but in slightly different form) in other areas of the British Isles, and what seems to be a distinctive culture may simply be a modification imposed by the nature of the chalk itself. Most of the methods which have been described here are scientific methods, and archaeology has claims to being considered a science, not only because it calls on these methods but because of its whole approach to the past and of the systematic way in which archaeological evidence is handled. None the less, archaeology can never be an exact science, and its ultimate aims, which demand a sympathetic understanding of man as man, are beyond the range of purely descriptive or formulating method. There is indeed a danger, especially in the study of European prehistory, that these ultimate aims may suffer if the preoccupation with techniques and technology in archaeology, which seems to be increasing, is not kept in proportion.

Archaeologists study people and peoples in the past. Their study is ultimately history, using evidence other than documentary. It is, in another aspect, cultural anthropology. But the very mention of these disciplines must remind the archaeologist of the special deficiencies in his evidence, of which he is ever conscious, the yawning gaps which can never be filled.

What is lacking is, above all, communication. The prehistoric past is silent. With all his battery of test-tubes and machines to call upon, although he adds to his scientific methods year by year, the archaeologist finally needs more than the collection of verifiable facts which they can provide, if he is to interpret the past. A study of the trees is necessary: he must also contrive to see the wood. Beyond the tools, the houses, the burial-deposits, he must strive for a glimpse of the men and women whose very names are unknown. From every phase of human activity much has vanished without a trace, and from prehistory especially all words are absent. Imagination, therefore, is necessary over and above method in approaching prehistory.

3

The achievements of archaeology

The starting point

Scientific archaeology is still a comparatively young discipline, but already its achievements in contributing to knowledge have been considerable. The accumulation of information was already large by the end of the nineteenth century, and through its interpretation in the years since then a great deal has been revealed about the origins and development of many elements in human culture. Archaeologists have studied the most diverse objects and commodities; like Lewis Carroll's Walrus, they 'talk of many things, of shoes and ships and sealing-wax, of cabbages and kings'. But perhaps the chief achievement of the new science has been its contribution to our knowledge not only of the origins but of the very nature of human culture.

The foundation of modern archaeology was, as we have already seen, the discovery of the antiquity of man. Any account of archaeological achievement must first take account of work on the most remote periods of human history, not only because it is convenient to deal with the material in chronological order, but because of the primary importance of this work in helping our understanding of the whole subject. It is convenient also because there must inevitably be different approaches to periods for which there is no contemporary written evidence anywhere in the world (this has been termed 'primary prehistory'), to periods for which there is some contemporary documentation but not in the part of the world being studied, and to periods and cultures which have contemporary written documents which are too few to give an adequate picture without the complementary use of material evidence.

The whole of the Palaeolithic – the Old Stone Age – belongs to the period before the beginnings of writing anywhere, and the material of the earlier or Lower Palaeolithic is particularly intractable. It must be admitted that in spite of a century's diligent researches not a great deal, in general terms, has been added to what was known of the beginning of man in the time of Boucher de Perthes. Research has proceeded on two main lines. Archaeologists have worked on the earliest identifiable man-made implements, while zoologists and anthropologists have tackled the difficult problem of the evolution of man.

The rocks of which our earth is made bear within them, in the form of fossils, the evidence for the slow elaboration (during a vast period of up to two thousand million years) of the forms of living beings, from the marvellously simple to the marvellously complex. Man makes a very late appearance on the scene, as one of the higher primates, and the details of his ancestry are still a matter of difficulty and dispute. The matter is one for anthropological rather than archaeological research, and it is sufficient to say here that in the present state of knowledge the most likely line of human evolution seems to be traceable in Africa and through the medium of a monkey-like creature who has been labelled *Australopithecus*. Quite recently, news has been coming of important discoveries made in the Olduvai Gorge in Tanzania. Here in 1959 Dr Leakey discovered bones of a creature intermediate between *Australopithecus* and Man, closely associated with primitive stone tools. This creature has been classified as *Zinjanthropus Boiseii*. More extensive investigations on and near the site have revealed tools, hearths, the remains possibly of rough stone windbreaks, and bones of a much more man-like creature, *Homo habilis*. It is at present uncertain if *Zinjanthropus* actually used or made tools. *Homo habilis,* who did, walked erect, had man-like (but stronger) hands and feet, and conformed in most respects to the description of Man, except that his skull capacity was relatively small. The evidence for tool-making is, however, from the archaeologist's point of view, definitive. For although the anthropologist may find it difficult to define man, the archaeologist has a simple criterion: the manufacture and use of tools.

By the time (geologically very recent) that archaeology comes fully into question, two distinct types of human stock are recognizable, one of which, represented by Neanderthal man, became extinct during the Palaeolithic period. As to the distinction between the two stocks, that again is a matter of dispute, one view holding that they are generically distinct, the more extreme contrary view being that they are simply intra-racial variants. At any rate, man as such hardly makes his appearance before the Quaternary era, the last major

76

division of geological time, and the shortest, being of the order of a million years. Two principal sub-divisions are recognized in the Quaternary: the Pleistocene, a period of recurrent Ice Ages with warm inter-glacial periods, and the Holocene or Recent period. The last stage of the Tertiary era, immediately before the Pleistocene, is termed the Pliocene.

The archaeologist's difficulty for this period lies in the fact that man was born naked into the world. A creature with an intelligence and a soul found himself an animal in a world of raw nature, inheriting nothing save his physical and intellectual attributes. All the complex paraphernalia of human culture that we know had to be won, painfully, courageously, and step by step, from the changing natural environment. It is man's unique ability to transmit his experience – not only physically through the inheritance of instinct, as animals in the main do, but by communication and tradition – that has enabled him to build up such an elaborate extra-corporeal adaptation to his world. But it is easy to imagine that at the very beginning of the process of tool-making, men may for long periods of time have used or even fashioned implements without leaving any clear record for the archaeologist to read.

If an early man picked up the branch of a tree to use it as a club, even allowing for an accident of preservation by which the branch may have survived for hundreds of thousands of years, there is nothing about a natural piece of wood to show that it was ever used as an implement; or if a man has broken a pebble to provide a sharp cutting edge, there may be no way of distinguishing the simple broken stone from the millions of pebbles which have been broken by natural agencies. It is only when a modicum of elaboration and skill has been applied in the making of an implement that it becomes recognizable as certainly the work of man.

The Palaeolithic phase

The earliest men of whom the archaeologist as such can be aware, therefore, are those who have left the earliest undeniably man-made tools. It is precisely on this point of distinguishing the work of man from the operation of natural forces that many controversies have turned in the past century. In Britain, for example, claims have been made from time to time of discoveries of implements in deposits of very early (Pliocene or Lower Pleistocene) date. Flints from Tertiary gravels in Kent have been described as 'eoliths' ('dawn-stones') and the late Mr Reid Moir of Ipswich claimed to distinguish not only humanly worked flints, but work in several different cultural traditions, in deposits of Lower Pleistocene age underlying the crag deposits of East Anglia. These claims have been challenged on various technical grounds and have not been generally accepted.

The oldest human artefacts so far identified with reasonable certainty are crudely flaked pebbles and lumps of rock which have been found in geological deposits of Lower Pleistocene date in various parts of Africa. These primitive chopping tools may have been used for tearing and cutting the skins of animals. Outside Africa no implements of so early a date have been identified with certainty.

The geological phase known as the Middle Pleistocene covers a period which in Europe was occupied by two major glaciations (the second and third Ice Ages, named Mindel and Riss) and a long interglacial period between them. For this immensely long stretch of time evidence for the work of man has been found in all quarters of the Old World. Again the evidence consists of the bare and simple stone tools. It must be remembered that the landscapes in which the Lower Palaeolithic peoples hunted or gathered their food have long since vanished in the geological changes which ensued. In northern Europe, for example, successive ice-sheets, slowly spreading down from the north, and as slowly retreating northward again, have altered or obliterated features of the landscape, gathering up and churning

Pebble tool from Olduvai

78

along flint implements, to deposit them in other sediments in melt-water perhaps hundreds of miles from the place where they were first lost. The stone tools of the Middle Pleistocene exhibit a gradual technical improvement in one great group of implements known as the Chelles-Acheul cultures. These seem to have had their main centre in Africa and to have been brought into Europe at suitable climatic intervals when the ice-sheets were in withdrawal. The implements are mainly of the type known as 'hand axes': large, more or less multi-purpose, tools of flint or stone. Their development can be traced from the crude choppers of Lower Pleistocene type through a series of more and more carefully elaborated axes, until there appears a technical innovation (the use of a rounded piece of wood or a large bone instead of a hammer stone to strike off the flakes) – the feature which distinguishes what is termed the Acheulian phase of the hand-axe cultures. The hand-axe cultures extended from Africa as far as Europe and nearer Asia, including parts of India. Farther afield there were more or less contemporary 'cultures', distinguished by other, and generally cruder, types of stone tools, in northern Europe, in south-east Asia, in China, and in southern Africa.

In terms of duration, the period which has here been summarized in a few paragraphs comprises by far the greater part of man's history on earth. Plainly, human society throughout this immense stretch of time must have been at the most primitive stage of savagery, although there may have been simple developments in communication and in social organization which we cannot trace. All that can be traced is the painfully slow improvement in the techniques of manufacturing a few very simple types of stone tool. After the Lower Palaeolithic, changes can be seen to come more rapidly, and an accelerating rate of technical development makes each succeeding phase more and more complex.

'Eolith' from Igtham

Laurel leaf blade from Solutré

After the Riss Glaciation – the third of the four major glacial phases of climate in Europe – a greater variety appears in the types of stone tools used, and the number of separate traditions or cultures which can be identified increases. The hand axe ceases to be the predominant tool, and more specialized and often smaller implements make their appearance. This variety increases further after the beginning of the final (Würm) glaciation, and a very high degree of skill in flint-working is manifest in some of the cultures of the Upper Palaeolithic, especially in the beautiful large laurel leaf shaped blades of the Solutrean culture of south-west and south central Europe at this period, with their fine rippled finish.

The number of human skulls or other bones which have been found in deposits of Palaeolithic age is tiny in comparison to the period of time involved, and the number found directly associated with flint implements is smaller by far, so that final conclusions about the physical characteristics of Palaeolithic man are not yet possible. Two main groups of fossil humans have been distinguished, however, one being ancestral to the present human race and the other (biologically more specialized) having become extinct towards the end of the Pleistocene period. The second, extinct, group was responsible for a great many of the Lower and Middle Palaeolithic implements which have been found. This group in turn may be sub-divided, but it is chiefly represented by the type known as Neanderthal man, whose remains have been found in various parts of Europe and in the East Mediterranean area. The characteristics which distinguish Neanderthal man from the ancestors of the present human race are mainly revealed in the form of the skull, which is quite distinct from the form of ape skulls but differs from modern human skulls in the heavy brow-ridges over the eyes, the massively built thick-chinned jaw, the low dome, and other minor features, all of which seem adapted to the muscular development necessary for very powerful chewing action. It is not certain whether fertile inter-breeding between Neanderthal man and the ancestors of modern man was possible but fairly recent evidence from two areas (Palestine, and Ehringsdorf in Germany) suggests that the clear distinction between the two stocks may not be as sharp as it was once thought to be. Other extinct human types, also specialized and more or less closely resembling Neanderthal man, have been identified in different parts of the world, including China (near Peking), Java, and Rhodesia.

Archaeology's chief achievement for the earlier part of the Palaeolithic period, in short, has been simply to show that man – more than one kind of man – existed in those early millennia, and was already manufacturing his equipment for dealing with an environment which underwent extreme changes in that enormous span of time. The men and women themselves, and their way of life, however, remain shadowy. For the later stages of the Palaeolithic it becomes possible to fill in more details. The evidence from the finds indicates that caves were being used as permanent habitations; more and more evidence becomes available on the hunting methods and gear employed in the search for food; evidence is available from the end of the Palaeolithic for the primitive tent-like structures erected by hunters of reindeer and other game in their camps, and finally a great deal of information (again about the later ages of the Palaeolithic period) is supplied by the most remarkable manifestation of the culture of our remote ancestors, their art.

Since the first discoveries in the late nineteenth century, diligent investigation has by now brought to light thousands of examples of painting, engraving, drawing, and sculpture dating from the end of the last, or Würm, glaciation onwards. How far back the tradition of human art extends beyond the earliest known examples is of course uncertain, but in view of the fact that early examples of art can survive only under extremely favourable conditions, it seems reasonable to assume that the evidence we have by no means tells the beginning of the story. The most astonishing thing about even the oldest examples of Palaeolithic art which survive is their liveliness and apparent sophistication. The favourite subjects of Palaeolithic man were the animals he knew, and especially those he hunted. Perhaps the earliest technique employed was engraving, with a flint point on pieces of stone, antler, or bone and also on the walls of caves. Such engravings often capture in a few lines the life and movement of an animal, but the most impressive depictions of animals are carried out on a large scale, in painted colour, on the walls of caves. Some caves have large numbers of these paintings, and form astonishingly vivid prehistoric art galleries in themselves. The best examples so far known are concentrated in regions of limestone caves north and south of the Pyrenees, and are most splendidly represented by the cave of Lascaux in southern France and the cave of Altamira in northern Spain. The fauna of the paintings in itself is interesting: many species of animals are represented which have since become either extinct altogether or extinct in the areas where the paintings are found. Bas-reliefs such as the frieze of horses at Cap Blanc in France, carved from the rock of the cave wall, also occur, but are much rarer. Animals are also represented in small carvings or modellings in the round, but in this medium there is an interesting group of female figurines with the sexual parts greatly exaggerated. One of the most famous of these (in the Vienna Museum) is known as the 'Venus of Willendorf', and the group as a whole is often referred to as venuses.

The 'Venus of Willendorf'

This art gives us a remarkable glimpse of the world of later Palaeolithic man – the world of hunters whose whole life was bound up with the creatures they pursued or feared. Horses, bison, and mammoths were among the animals with which they were familiar. It seems likely that in part at least the purpose of the art was magical; that by representing the successful hunt the hunters sought to bring it about. This view is perhaps supported by the fact that animals of the chase are occasionally found carved on the hunter's weapons themselves – harpoons and spear-throwers. Such weapons or instruments have survived in considerable numbers from the closing stages of the Palaeolithic period, especially from the culture known as the Magdalenian (after the site of La Madeleine in southern France). Tools and weapons of bone, ivory, and antler, as well as an increasing variety of stone implements, are known from this late culture of hunters who lived preying on the reindeer herds which followed the retreating ice-sheets of the final glaciation northwards.

Cave painting of a bison, Altamira

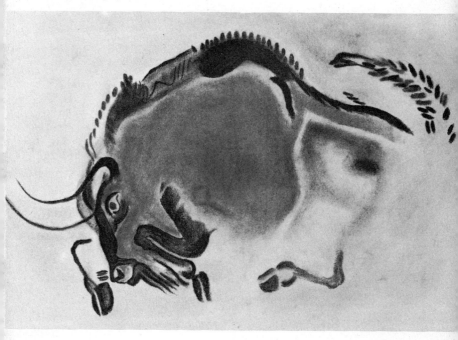

Sculpture of bisons, Le Tuc d'Audoubert

Stag engraved on perforated staff, Grotte des Hotcaux

Mammoth hunters' camp, Dolní Věstonice

The Mesolithic phase

Palaeolithic cultures are becoming increasingly known in other parts of the world, but the sequence of events has been most fully worked out in Europe, where investigation has been continuous for more than a century. Here the special circumstances which developed after the final Ice Age led archaeologists, who had at first distinguished only an Old Stone Age and a New Stone Age, to recognize a distinctive intermediate phase, the Middle Stone Age or Mesolithic period. The governing factor was a fundamental change in the environment of late Palaeolithic man as the result of the climatic improvement when the ice slowly withdrew. This was the growth of dense forests over the once open landscapes where mammoth and reindeer had been hunted. The forest called for a radical adaptation of the economy and equipment of primitive man; he had to devise tree-felling and wood-working implements and change his hunting and fishing techniques to deal with different, and on the whole smaller, game. This change in environment took place gradually, and the adaptation was correspondingly slow and did not involve a complete break with Upper Palaeolithic tradition. Many types of implement, including the bone harpoon, continued to be made, but many were modified in form. The manufacture of very small flint implements, which had been increasing towards the very end of the Palaeolithic, now became common. Some of these were arrowheads for bringing down small game, others points for mounting in wood or other material to form a composite weapon, others served a variety of purposes – scraping, boring, gouging, and all the simple manual operations performed by people who worked in wood, flesh, skin, and bone.

Mesolithic cultures have been most intensively studied and are best known in northern Europe. One of the most thoroughly investigated sites is at Star Carr in Yorkshire, excavated by Professor Clark. Here, when the post-glacial forests were still developing in northern Europe, Mesolithic hunters had their summer camp on a lake shore. Most of the activities of a hunters' camp were traced by skilful excavation: the hunting itself, revealed by weapons of the chase and by the bones of deer and smaller game, including birds of various species; the felling of birch trees and the removal of the bark which was used for flooring the camp and for various other purposes; the skinning and the preparation of the flesh, and finally even the dances or magical rites for ensuring the success of the hunt – indicated by deer skulls prepared to be worn as masks, presumably in a dance where men imitated the behaviour of both hunters and hunted. Star Carr is an important early Mesolithic site. Numbers of sites of a related but in the main somewhat later culture have been investigated on the far side of the North Sea (large parts of which at this time were dry land or marsh), and from one of the sites the culture has been named the Maglemose culture. Maglemose hunters and fishers, like their Palaeolithic forebears, had their own art style; on the whole more abstract and less spectacular in scale and achievement than Palaeolithic art. It consists of stylized linear designs engraved on small objects, and of a series of very impressive small animals carved in the round from amber.

The remains at Star Carr or at Maglemose sites in Denmark give a fairly vivid impression of hunting communities, small and primitive but vigorous, winning their food from forest, lake, and stream during the long period roughly from 8000 to 4000 B.C. In other parts of Europe, Mesolithic cultures vary from one major geographical region to another, from coastal squatters (who were largely gatherers rather than hunters of food) living on shellfish, to the spartan survivors of the Palaeolithic hunters of the tundra, who continued to hunt the reindeer in Arctic regions. But all the Mesolithic peoples had this in

Maglemosian axe in antler sleeve (opposite) *and carved amber animal*

87

common: that they had as yet no positive control over their environment; they were dependent for their food on what nature of itself produced, on wild animals, birds, and fish, on wild herbs, berries, and fruit. In such circumstances their numbers must have been extremely small indeed compared with modern populations. In a hunting or gathering economy, quite a small group of people needs a large territory for its sustenance, and it must be prepared to move about following the seasons and the game. None the less, the increasing diversity of specialized implements, the ready adaptability to changing conditions, the new control over the world of nature which is shown by the domestication of dogs for the chase, all these indicate that Mesolithic man, unknowingly, was equipping himself for the major revolution in human affairs which was to come.

The beginning of the Neolithic phase

If archaeology's first major achievement was to demonstrate the antiquity of man, its second surely was its revealing of the very foundation of civilization. The Neolithic period is not simply the third sub-division of the Stone Age: it is marked by what was perhaps the most important economic revolution in human history – the beginning of agriculture and the domestication of food animals. The importance of this is in its effect in providing a consistent and greatly increased food supply. This meant that considerably larger populations could be supported, and that people could live settled in one place. Equally important, there was a sufficient surplus so that not all the population need devote their energies to the providing of food; some could now devote themselves to specialized crafts or trade. This combination of settled habitation and specialization provided the conditions necessary for the first development of towns and cities, and thus for civilization.

Recent evidence seems to indicate that while the Neolithic revolution first took place in the Near East – in the valley of the Tigris-Euphrates and in the valley of the Nile – it occurred independently in other areas: in the Indus valley, the Yellow River valley, and three separate locations in America. Its origins are not yet known in great detail. It is believed that the wild grasses which were the ancestors of wheat and barley grew indigenously in the East Mediterranean area, and it may be that at first people living in a Mesolithic state of economy simply supplemented their diet by reaping these wild crops, and later came to see the advantage of returning some of the grain to the soil as seed. At any rate at an early date people living in Palestine, who lived by hunting, fishing, and gathering, began to make sickles, with flint teeth mounted in bone handles, which were certainly used for reaping some such crop, whether cultivated or wild. Other communities in Egypt and the Middle East cultivated plants and kept livestock – cattle, sheep, and pigs. They ground down the grain with the simplest type of mill, consisting of a large stone on which a small rubbing stone was pushed up and down – the 'saddle quern' – and they made pits or silos for storing the grain.

A Natufian sickle
(15" in length),
sickle flints
(2" in length)

Egyptian statuette of woman
grinding corn on a quern

Triticum boeoticum (wild)

Triticum monococcum (cultivated)

Triticum dicoccoides (wild)

Triticum dicoccum (Emmer, cultivated)

Triticum spelta (spelt, cultivated)

Triticum compactum (club wheat, cultivated)

Triticum aestivum (cultivated)

In Egypt, in Iraq, and in Iran special conditions favoured the development of permanent settlements. The soil was watered not principally by rain, but by irrigation, depending on the periodic floods of great rivers such as the Nile and the Tigris-Euphrates, which not only supplied water to the fields but also brought down fresh soil in the form of muddy sediments, thus every year restoring the fertility of the land. This enabled the primitive farmers to continue cultivating the same fields over and over again for generations without exhausting the soil, and surpluses were made available to allow increase in population and growing specialization. The area available for cultivation was extended by drawing off the river water in irrigation canals and ditches, watering and fertilizing larger and larger areas of land. Irrigation affected the soil in various ways. For one thing the great loss of water from shallow channels through evaporation in a hot climate could lead to a marked increase in salinity, since the salts held in solution or suspension were deposited as the water evaporated, and too much salinity could ultimately render the soil infertile. But by and large the effect of the canals and channels was to create an artificial environment – to some extent an artificial climate – with a range of conditions which favoured both human and natural experiment. It was in such conditions that plants as well as animals were domesticated and new strains produced. At any rate the food supply was assured, and since agriculture of its nature imposes providence, surpluses were stored in the granaries and provision could be made for those who were not directly engaged in food-winning. In these conditions urban development began, and it seems reasonably certain that the oldest cities were in this part of the world.

The results of carbon-dating suggest that Neolithic Jericho was already in existence by about 7000 B.C.; but this, although walled and having an architectural character, was little more than a village in size – true cities, with a real division of labour, came into being much later, in the alluvial valleys of great river-systems. Here only was a sufficiently large-scale accumulation of surplus food – in centralized granaries – possible, here where the river acted at once as a highway and as a renewer of fertility. Here communities grew which included not only farmers but craftsmen and priests. The products of the craftsmen found markets far afield, in less well situated agricultural communities who yet produced a small surplus of food which they could exchange for specialized and useful manufactures. Once the process had got under way in each of these valleys, therefore, wealth – in its primary form of grain – began flowing in from

Ears of wild and cultivated wheat   91

Hypostyle hall, Luxor temple

an ever wider area, more and more non-food-producing people could
be supported at the centre to devote their time and skill to the
improvement of technology; centralization of wealth, of population,
of power, all went together to produce the growth of cities and of
civilization. In this way centralized civilized empires grew up in the
valleys of the Nile, the Tigris-Euphrates, the Indus, and later in the
Yellow River. Growing from simple peasant communities, they went
on to express materially the differences in power and wealth which
were becoming more and more extreme. Mud, and the grain it produced
with its annual renewal, were the foundations of civilization; the
granary, the accumulation of real wealth, was the basis of both temple

and palace. The ancient civilizations, therefore, have a number of features in common. Each, however, developed in its own way and has a character of its own.

Urban development

The period in which urban civilization developed was one in which the human race made great technical advances. Lower and Middle Palaeolithic man had had a very poor technical equipment – a few general-purpose stone tools, and an ability to make use of fire. In the Upper Palaeolithic and the Mesolithic periods a much more versatile equipment was available: special techniques had been developed for working bone and antler; flint implements were produced in variety to meet different purposes, and composite tools of wood or bone mounted with small flints were made; some elaborate or highly specialized equipment had been devised, such as fishing nets and hooks. With the coming of agriculture and the new techniques that went with it, man's technical equipment and knowledge greatly increased. Elementary mechanical and chemical principles were applied by Neolithic man. He could bore holes in stone by using abrasive and a drill rotated by means of a string. He could change the chemical nature of clay by heating it to produce pottery or bricks. He could polish stone with abrasives to provide more efficient axes and other wood-working tools. And, in place of the skin or turf shelters of Upper Palaeolithic and Mesolithic times, he learned to make permanent houses of wood, reeds, mud, brick, or stone, depending on the materials available. The spinning and weaving of wool is attested from almost all Neolithic cultures by the finding of spindle-whorls, loom-weights, and weaving-combs.

Neolithic man also acquired greater control over fire, learning how to produce higher temperatures by means of simple ovens or kilns. This art led, at quite an early date in the Middle East, to the ability to melt or fuse metals and (more important, since metals are not commonly found in the native state in nature) to the ability, almost simultaneously achieved, to extract copper from its ores. Metal, being malleable and fusible, is much more versatile than stone and for a great many purposes much more efficient. Its possession, some understanding of its properties, and some elementary metallurgical techniques were of great importance in the growth of civilization.

In a few limited areas in the world, therefore, in the period roughly from 6000 to 3000 B.C. cities and centralized administrations came into being. They depended on agriculture, but they gradually had sufficient numbers of non-agricultural workers to give them a true urban character. The population included not only builders, carpenters, and later potters, metal-workers, and other productive workers, but also kings, priests, and administrators. The administrators were responsible in the course of time for a further important contribution to the development of civilization. They were the store-keepers of the stocks of grain and other valuables which formed the capital wealth of temples and palaces; as centralized rule increased, they were responsible also for tax-gathering and census-taking. In other words, they had to keep accounts, and in lands whose whole prosperity depended on periodic river-flooding and an observance of the correct season for sowing crops, they were responsible for keeping accurate records of the duration of the seasons and of the year. Beginning with simple tally systems, symbols devised for use on official seals, the symbols or simplified pictures of objects which they used as records, and the observations which they made of natural phenomena in calculating the seasons of the year, these ancient administrators gradually, one generation after another, worked out the systems which led to the beginnings of writing, mathematics, and

Amratian stone vessel, Egyptian, c.4000 B.C.

A hieroglyphic inscription, Egypt

astronomy. By about 3000 B.C. forms of writing were established in Egypt and Sumer, and were already being used for documents other than simple tallies and accounts. With this development – the beginning of history – archaeology ceases to be the only source of information on the cultures of the Middle East. And, while the use of writing did not come to Europe and many other parts of the world until long afterwards, documentary evidence from the Middle East can sometimes help in the study, and especially the dating, of European cultures which were in contact, by trade or otherwise, with the East Mediterranean area.

Archaeology and ancient history

In spite of the fact that many of them had copious historical documents of their own, the civilizations of the ancient world, other than the comparatively late civilizations of Greece and Rome, were almost unknown two centuries ago. Archaeology has opened up to knowledge not only the whole of human prehistory, but a great deal of ancient history as well. This is because our knowledge of Greek and Roman history comes to us by tradition, by the copying and re-copying of the documents which has been continuous in the West since ancient times. But the documents of Egypt, of Sumer, of Babylon, of the Hittites, of Mycenae, and of other civilizations have been literally dug up, along with the tombs, temples, palaces, houses, and chattels of those cultures as the result of archaeological research. The documents, in fact, survive only because many of them, fortunately, are inscribed on durable materials – on tablets of clay or on the walls of monumental buildings. Their decipherment and interpretation is not, strictly speaking, the archaeologist's function, although the archaeologist who deals with inscriptions will as a matter of course be as familiar as possible with the languages in which they are written – but it is he who has made them available for linguistic scholars and historians. As may be imagined, it is a difficult and slow task to decipher writings in strange scripts and in ancient, often unknown, languages, and many ancient writings have been found which still cannot be read. But the diligent spade of the archaeologist has altered the whole perspective of ancient history, as well as putting history itself in the perspective of prehistory. The story of human civilization can no longer seem to begin with the Greek city states (or, to

take an equally out-dated but non-European viewpoint, with the Shang Dynasty in Honan) and to be a simple tale of the ambitions of rulers, of war and politics. Behind Classical Greece there was Mycenae, behind Mycenae there was Knossos, behind Knossos there was Egypt, and behind Egypt there were hunters who learned to cultivate plants and to keep and breed animals.

If the discovery of Palaeolithic cultures has altered man's view of himself in one way, the discovery of ancient civilizations has done so in another. The widespread romantic interest which was aroused at an early stage in the discovery has already been mentioned; an interest partly composed of enthusiasm for the strange and forgotten arts and monuments which were being revealed, partly of awe at the oblivion which had befallen mighty civilizations. But these things, in a hundred and fifty years of discovery, have come to be taken for granted, while they have enriched the culture of the world. The great monuments of the past have become familiar – not only the pyramids of Egypt, which were always visible to the traveller, but the ziggurats and palaces of Iraq, the temples of Angkor, and the cities of Aztec Mexico.

A ziggurat, Ur

Egyptian sculpture of the Old Kingdom.
State pair statue of Mycerinus and his Queen: IV *Dynasty*

99

Archaeology's view of human history

Civilization and literacy took thousands of years to spread from their centres of origin, and until quite recent times there were many parts of the world which they had not reached. But some of their effects were far-reaching, and their very existence in one part of the world introduces some complexity into the study of other parts. The area where this period, from about 3000 B.C. onward, has been most intensively studied is Europe, and the knowledge which archaeology has provided on the ancestors of the European peoples may stand as an example of what it has achieved or can achieve in other regions of the earth. This knowledge is extensive and detailed, and much of the main outline of the story is clear, although a very great deal yet remains to be understood.

Neolithic cultures and economy made their way into prehistoric Europe along two main routes – up the valley of the Danube into Central Europe from the Near Eastern cradle of civilization, and westward along the Mediterranean from the same centres. The movement, which was probably one of migrant farmers and herders, seems from the evidence of radio-carbon dating to have been under way in the fifth millennium B.C., but to have been quite slow in its progress. Very early Neolithic cultures can be traced in the Balkans and the East Mediterranean islands – cultures of village or cave dwellers who planted cereals, kept cattle, sheep, and pigs, and stored their grain in pits, but who also supplemented their diet by hunting and fishing. Over an enormous area of Central Europe a group of remarkably uniform cultures has been traced, which represents the earliest Neolithic settlers who entered by the Danubian route. These people were predominantly tillage farmers. They sought out and settled one particular type of easily cultivated soil – the löss – and they lived in quite large villages of rectangular houses. Like most early Neolithic peoples in Europe they seem to have been migrant, having no way of restoring fertility to the soil, but moving on after it had been exhausted by their hoe-cultivation. They had characteristic types of pottery, they used polished stone axes, and they had querns for grinding the corn. Their villages were fenced or (in later times, at least) fortified, and there was some long-distance trade from village to village – sometimes in pots, sometimes in especially useful types of stone, and sometimes in ornaments (*Spondylus* shells from the Mediterranean were traded far north into Europe).

Neolithic polished axe

The westward spread of Neolithic cultures along the Mediterranean brought the knowledge and practice of farming to southern Italy and Sicily, to the West Mediterranean islands, North Africa, and Spain. The movement into Spain and from there northward has not yet been clarified, but there was a large Western Neolithic province, distinguished by a number of types in common, which bordered the Danubian Neolithic more or less along the Rhine. This western

Reconstruction of a neolithic village at Köln-Lindenthal

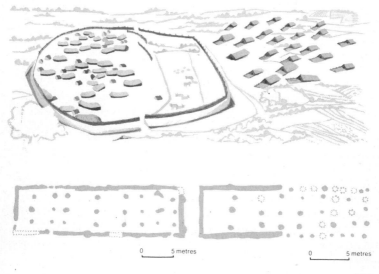

0   5 metres   0   5 metres

Reconstructed neolithic house, Lough Gur, Co. Limerick

province shared a characteristic type of pot – round-bottomed, leathery in texture, and often shouldered. Such pottery was made by the first farming communities who came (by sea) to Great Britain and Ireland. These were communities who practised mixed farming – tillage and herding – and who built rectangular or round wooden houses. Like the other European Neolithic peoples, they showed a preference for light easily-worked soils, chalk or limestone, free from dense forest. Together with the new economy, they brought with them what was surely a religion or a religious idea of Mediterranean origin. This is indicated by the most impressive monuments which follow the distribution of the Western Neolithic: the great barrows or cairns covering burials, usually collective burials, which are distributed along the Atlantic shores of Europe. Most of these tombs are megalithic; that is to say, the mound covers a chamber or galley constructed of massive stones. In the British Isles, at any rate, the earliest Neolithic burial mounds seem to be long barrows, chambered and unchambered; but round barrows – covering a chamber approached by a covered passage – which have much closer Mediterranean parallels, were also constructed in Neolithic times. The passage graves, which are confined to the western parts of the British Isles, but are found also in the Iberian Peninsula, in Western France, and in Scandinavia, are remarkable not only because of their truly monumental scale and construction, but because of their art – a rich ornament of zig-zags, spirals, concentric circles, and other semi-geometric motives, engraved on the great stones of tombs in

Entrance stone, Newgrange (top)
Cairns at Loughcrew, Co. Meath

103

France, Ireland, Wales, and Scotland. Similar motives appear in Iberia, not on the structure of the tombs, but on stone plaques found in them, and not scattered in haphazard fashion, but organized in what appear to be stylized representations of a female figure – perhaps the goddess of death.

Knowledge of metallurgy appears to have been diffused along the same two main routes into Europe from the Middle East, at a much later date, and early in the second millennium B.C. rich Early Bronze Age cultures came into being in Spain, in Central Europe and in the British Isles. These were characterised by a remarkable increase in long-distance trade, and, in Central Europe at least, apparently by a stratification of society and the appearance of hill-top strongholds dominating the trade routes and the pastoral countryside. Products of workshops of the civilized East Mediterranean were traded across Europe as far as Ireland and Denmark, in exchange apparently for gold, copper, amber, and other materials, probably including salt. With the Bronze Age the culture of Europe becomes much more complex and diversified, each region having its distinctive culture. But the general pattern is clear: a multitude of local cultures, connected by trade with one another and, more and more, with the spreading urban civilizations to the south-east.

Distribution of faience beads in Europe

This condition lasted until towards the end of the second millennium B.C. Then, about the twelfth century B.C., the diffusion of civilization received a severe check, and the whole of Europe entered into a phase of unrest and upheaval. Mycenae and its power were overthrown by invaders from the north; invaders from the north, too, overthrew the Hittite Empire in Asia Minor; Egypt was in decline, and her coasts were ravaged by pirates and other attackers. Many centres of civilization in the East Mediterranean relapsed into barbarism, and in many the records cease for a time.

By the time, about the middle of the first millennium B.C. that this period of confusion is drawing to an end, Europe is emerging into the light of history, and archaeology begins to be aware of at least the names of the peoples whose cultures it is dealing with. The use of iron has now reached Central Europe from the south-east, and the aristocratic agricultural societies of the Celts occupy the heart of the Continent. Brilliant art-styles in metalwork distinguish the later phases of prehistory on the Continent, and each of them can be attributed, at least tentatively, to races or nations whose names we know from later records: the splendid bronzework of the Nordic Bronze Age to the ancestors of the Germans, the rich goldwork and fantastic animal style of the East European steppe to the Scythians,

A Hallstatt sword

105

the elaborate stylized adaptations of animal and vegetable ornament in West and Central Europe to the Celts, and so on. Finally, the expansion of Roman power and the barbarian resistance to it can be traced in the material record. The Roman invasion of Britain, for example, is marked by a series of monuments: on the one hand the British hill forts which resisted the invasion; on the other, the rectangular military camps of the invaders. The struggle and the later relations between the two peoples can be studied in detail through excavation, sometimes in dramatic detail, as in Sir Mortimer Wheeler's excavation of the Maiden Castle hill fort, where the storming of the gate was marked by the skeletons of those killed in the battle and hurriedly buried, one with a Roman ballista bolt still embedded in his backbone.

Archaeology has revealed and is revealing much not only about prehistoric cultures but also about societies in protohistoric or full historic periods – about the Greeks, the Etruscans, the Goths, the Huns, the Anglo-Saxons, and even about late medieval society in Europe. By examining briefly what archaeological research has done in enlarging knowledge of periods and cultures such as these, where we are dealing with peoples whom we can also apprehend through history, we can, perhaps, best judge the value of archaeology for the study of the prehistoric past, and assess its potentialities and its limitations. It is limited by the nature of the evidence it employs. It can tell only the story of society as a whole (and even that not in full), not the deeds of lawgivers, kings, and captains; and the social history it can provide is one-sided – ideas and beliefs can only be inferred. But although archaeological evidence must be interpreted to give it meaning, and interpretation can all too easily go astray, the evidence in itself is more factual, more true, than many historical documents, which were as often written to persuade or to deceive as they were to expound the plain facts. Even in full historical periods, archaeology can often restore a balance by acting as an advocate for the inarticulate. A literate people in contact with an illiterate people, after all, has an overwhelming advantage in history: the one can present its case and the other cannot. So, if we learn about the Gauls or the Germans only from the writings of Romans, who were their enemies, we are bound to be presented with at the best a misunderstanding and at the worst a misrepresentation of them. But the spade is indifferent to the opinions or prejudices which lay behind the objects it digs up. Finally, archaeology can add a new dimension to history, giving it depth by providing for study not merely what men have said

but what they have made, concrete evidence of the way they have lived and the things that have pleased them. The magnificent East Anglian jewellery from Sutton Hoo tells us something about the Anglo-Saxons which cannot be glimpsed from the meagre records of the Dark Ages, just as the sculptures and painted glass of Chartres Cathedral illuminate for us the mind of the Christian Middle Ages.

Archaeology, then, is a discipline which has already contributed greatly and continues to contribute to our knowledge and understanding of man. If it suffers from all the weaknesses, it also benefits from all the considerable value of circumstantial evidence. However imperfectly, it is restoring what had seemed lost in oblivion, the whole story of humanity's struggle towards the empire of the earth.

The Sutton Hoo pursemount

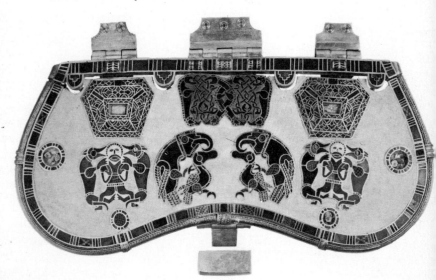

Index